Naac

D0368815

James Herriot's

Animal Stories

ALSO BY JAMES HERRIOT

All Creatures Great and Small
All Things Bright and Beautiful
All Things Wise and Wonderful
The Lord God Made Them All
Every Living Thing
James Herriot's Yorkshire
James Herriot's Dog Stories
The Best of James Herriot
James Herriot's Cat Stories
James Herriot's Favorite Dog Stories

FOR CHILDREN

Moses the Kitten
Only One Woof
The Christmas Day Kitten
Bonny's Big Day
Blossom Comes Home
The Market Square Dog
Oscar, Cat-About-Town
Smudge, the Little Lost Lamb
James Herriot's Treasury for Children

James Herriot's

Animal Stories

With an Introduction by Jim Wight and
Illustrations by Lesley Holmes

St. Martin's Press ✖ New York

NOTE

Stories in this volume first appeared in *All Creatures Great and Small, All Things Bright and Beautiful, All Things Wise and Wonderful, The Lord God Made Them All,* and *Every Living Thing.*

JAMES HERRIOT'S ANIMAL STORIES. Copyright © 1997 by The James Herriot Partnership. Introduction © 1997 by Jim Wight. Illustrations © 1997 by Lesley Holmes. All rights reserved. Printed in China. For information, address St. Martin's Press, 175 Fifth Avenue, New York, N.Y. 10010.

www.stmartins.com

Library of Congress Cataloging-in-Publication Data

Herriot, James
    [Animal stories]
    James Herriot's animal stories / James Herriot ; illustrations by
  Lesley Holmes.
       p. cm.
    ISBN 978-1-250-05935-2 (hardcover)
    1. Herriot, James. 2. Veterinarians—England—Yorkshire—
Biography. 3. Domestic animals—England—Yorkshire—Anecdotes.
I. Title.
    SF613.H44A3 1997
    636.089'092—dc21
    [B]
                                     9713863

St. Martin's Press books may be purchased for educational, business, or promotional use. For information on bulk purchases, please contact the Macmillan Corporate and Premium Sales Department at 1-800-221-7945, extension 5442, or write to specialmarkets@macmillan.com.

First published in Great Britain by Michael Joseph Ltd

Second U.S. Edition: May 2015

10 9 8 7 6 5 4 3 2 1

Contents

Introduction

by Jim Wight

Tommy Banks, one of my father's oldest and most respected farm clients, looked down at the small boy standing confidently in his farmyard, shiny new boots in stark contrast to his own. Mr. Banks was observing a seasoned and highly experienced "veterinary assistant," a veteran of hundreds of farm visits whose very bearing exuded pride and dedication to his job. I was that boy.

A kindly smile spread over the farmer's face. "Are you going to be a vet like your dad?" he asked. He was unprepared for the swift, indignant reply.

"I *am* a vet!" I said, drawing myself up to my full height—a few inches under three feet. Having attained the heady age of four years old, I considered myself to be a fully qualified veterinary surgeon. I could not understand why Mr. Banks was laughing.

The source of my unshakable conviction that a

veterinary surgeon's life was the one for me was my father, James Alfred Wight, a man whose total dedication, love and enthusiasm for his job was transmitted down to me as a four-year-old child. I would consider nothing else for my future career and little did I realize that, so many years later, as James Herriot, my father would instill that same fascination for veterinary practice into the minds of millions of people.

The veterinary profession has never before been held in higher esteem. The modern child regards a life in veterinary medicine as a top priority when future careers are being considered, and James Herriot is largely responsible.

My father was my best friend, and since his death a day never goes by that I do not think of him; but I console myself with the knowledge that he has left us with wonderful memories of a bygone age, a vivid picture of a way of life that has disappeared but has been reborn so clearly and enjoyably through his incomparable skills as an observer of human nature and, of course, as a writer.

The stories in this book clearly illustrate James Herriot's gift of transporting the reader into his own world. We are there with him, sharing his triumphs and disappointments, just as he did, with the many fascinating characters who were part of his life and provided him with such unique material for his books. Lesley Holmes's beautiful illustrations brilliantly complement the stories, and help the reader to escape even deeper into James Herriot's world.

I, of course, do not remember James Herriot simply as an author, but more importantly as a friend, a veterinary surgeon, and a father second to none. He had a demanding and time-consuming job, but would always find time to spend with his children. My sister, Rosie, and I would listen, open-mouthed, to the magical stories he read aloud to us by H. Rider Haggard, H. G. Wells and many other great writers. My father was a great student of history, and we relived titanic struggles on distant Scottish battlefields and sailed with bold explorers to undiscovered lands. Closer to home we would laugh at the exploits of his veterinary colleagues, Siegfried and Tristan, and a host of other funny people that my father knew. We were, in fact, listening to the origins of *All Creatures Great and Small* from the mouth of the master storyteller himself who, many years later, would ensure that the world could share in our enjoyment.

One of the clear memories I have of a very happy childhood is of extreme cold. Winters in Yorkshire, in the 1940s, were a wonderful time for small children. There was plenty of snow and often in the mornings we would wake up to a white world—white outside and white inside. Number 23 Kirkgate, our first family home, later to become famous as "Skeldale House," was not a warm house, and the beautiful "Jack Frost" patterns on the windows, the perpetually moving curtains, and the icy stone-flagged corridors all bore testimony to the house's winter mood.

In those early years, James Herriot's life was hard. In many chapters in his books he refers to the inevitable night work, the jangling telephone summoning him to another crisis on a faraway farm at times when it seemed everyone in the world but he was asleep. I would often accompany him, day or night, in his primitive little heaterless cars, and in response to my cries of discomfort he would say, "Wiggle your toes, Jimmy. Clap your hands!" I had to learn to survive. I was James Herriot's first "veterinary assistant," opening gates, carrying bottles, or catching calves, sharing in his experiences of the tough Yorkshire farming community that was to provide such a great source of material for his future years as a writer.

Those early years were rough but, in my father's own words, "They were more fun," and when I think back to those days I do not feel cold; I feel a warmth born of a happy childhood with the finest of fathers.

Shortly after the memorial service for my father in York Minster I was asked if I would consider writing his biography. Having accepted such a challenge I determined that my first step would be to reread all the James Herriot books, not only to pick up a few tips from the master but also to attempt an analysis of the reasons for his phenomenal success. It soon became clear to me that attempting to put his writing "under the microscope" was a waste of time. I simply reread the stories and enjoyed them. My father never wished that his writing should be the subject of any close scrutiny. He intended that the stories should simply be read and enjoyed, and this clearly shows in his books.

A local farmer, having read one of the Herriot books—this was received with a genuine astonishment by my dad, who never thought that the local people would read and enjoy them—said that he thought it was "very good but it was all about *nowt!*" I know exactly what he was trying to say. James Herriot had the rare ability to turn everyday happenings into a compelling read with the use of uncomplicated words delivered with maximum effect. His stories are very largely about that fascinating subject, Human Nature, and they were written by one of life's keenest observers. He watched, he understood, and most importantly, he preserved in print the thoughts of a compassionate and humorous man. James Herriot's tales are not primarily about animals, they are about people.

Animal characters do, of course, figure prominently too. In the following pages you will encounter Tricki Woo, the little Pekingese whose generosity was responsible for a regular supply of succulent food hampers to the appreciative "Uncle Wight"—or, as it appeared in the books, "Uncle Herriot." The little dog that I remember so well was deeply hurt when his favorite uncle committed the elementary blunder of addressing a thank-you letter to "Master Tricki Woo" when, of course, the appropriate mode of address should have read "Tricki Woo, Esq." To my father's and the family's dismay, the stream of delicious foods promptly dried up, but a groveling letter of apology to the affronted little animal was graciously accepted and the crisis was averted.

Tricki Woo, Blossom the cow who refused to leave home, Herbert the orphan lamb with the indomitable will to live are all examples of James Herriot's gift of interweaving human qualities into his animal characters. It is, however, the vivid and large-as-life portrayal of the human characters themselves that is mainly responsible for James Herriot's success. Siegfried, Tristan, Calum, Granville Bennett, and many more have become household names, and these so-unforgettable individuals are brought to life through the skillful, descriptive talents of the writer.

Years ago, as a schoolboy, I was reading an action-packed paperback and my father said to me, "Jim, have you ever read the classics? Charles Dickens? Sir Walter Scott?"

"Too much descriptive stuff. Not enough action," was my schoolboy reply.

My father laughed. "I love descriptive bits, the way these great writers put you in the picture and carry you into their world."

I thought about this as a boy, but reading my father's books again has led me to realize that perhaps he learned so much from these famous authors because he himself possessed the gift of "setting the scene." Read James Herriot's stories and you are there with him. You will laugh with him, you may cry with him and, above all, after reading him you will feel good.

In February 1995, three days before he died, my father was reading *The White Company* by Sir Arthur Conan Doyle. Illness had taken its toll on him physically, but his mind remained as alert as ever. "What a terrific writer Conan Doyle was," he said. "I have read this book, I don't know how many times, but I'm enjoying it just as much this time round. The mark of a great writer."

My father could never understand the reasons for his success, but one thing I do know: On that day in February, this modest, unassuming man, that self-proclaimed "amateur at the writing game," had unwittingly identified himself with those literary giants he had admired so much as a boy. James Herriot's stories have been, and will be, read over and over again.

—YORKSHIRE, 1997

Herbert,
the Orphaned Lamb

I realized, quite suddenly, that spring had come. It was late March and I had been examining some sheep in a hillside fold. On my way down, in the lee of a small pine wood, I leaned my back against a tree and was aware, all at once, of the warm sunshine on my closed eyelids, the clamor of the larks, the muted sea-sound of the wind in the high branches. And although the snow still lay in long runnels behind the walls, and the grass was lifeless and winter-yellowed, there was the feeling of change.

It wasn't a warm spring but it was dry with sharp winds which fluttered the white heads of the snow-drops and bent the clumps of daffodils on the village greens. Soon the roadside banks would be bright with the fresh yellow of primroses.

I pondered a moment on the months ahead of me. In April came the lambing. It came in a great tidal wave, the most vivid and interesting part of the veterinary surgeon's year, the zenith of the annual cycle, and it came as it always does when we were busiest with our other work.

In the spring the livestock were feeling the effects of the long winter. Cows had stood for months in the same few feet of byre and were in dire need of fresh green grass and the sun on their backs, while their calves had very little resistance to disease. And just when we were wondering how we could cope with the coughs and colds and pneumonias, lambing would be upon us.

The odd thing is that for about ten months of the year, sheep hardly entered into the scheme of our lives; they were just woolly things on the hills. Then for the other two months they almost blotted out everything else. By the end of May most of the problems would have dried up and sheep became woolly things on the hills again

But in this first year I found a fascination in the work which has remained with me. Lambing had all the thrill and interest of calving without the hard labor. It was usually uncomfortable in that it was performed in the open; either in drafty pens improvised from straw bales and gates or more often out in the

fields. It didn't seem to occur to the farmers that the ewe might prefer to produce her family in a warm place or that the vet may not enjoy kneeling for an hour in his shirtsleeves in the rain.

And the lambs. All young animals are appealing but the lamb has been given an unfair share of charm. The moments come back; of a bitterly cold evening when I had delivered twins on a wind-scoured hillside; the lambs shaking their heads convulsively and within minutes one of them struggling upright and making its way, unsteady, knock-kneed, toward the udder while the other followed resolutely on its knees.

The shepherd, his purple, weather-roughened face almost hidden by the heavy coat which muffled him to his ears, gave a slow chuckle. "How the 'ell do they know?"

He had seen it happen thousands of times and he still wondered. So do I.

And another memory of two hundred lambs in a barn on a warm afternoon. We were inoculating them and there was no conversation because of the high-pitched protests of the lambs and the unremitting deep baa-ing from nearly a hundred ewes milling anxiously around outside. I couldn't conceive how these ewes could ever get their own families sorted out from that mass of almost identical little creatures. It would take hours.

It took about twenty-five seconds. When we had finished, we opened the barn doors and the outpouring lambs were met by a concerted rush of distraught mothers. At first the noise was deafening but it died away rapidly to an occasional bleat as the last stray was rounded up. Then neatly paired off, the flock headed calmly for the field.

On this particular morning, I had been called out to Rob Benson's farm. At the top of the grassy slope the pens, built of straw bales, formed a long row of square cubicles each holding a ewe with her lambs and I could see the farmer coming round the far end carrying two feeding buckets. He was hard at it; at this time of the year he didn't go to bed for about six weeks; he would maybe take off his boots and doze by the kitchen fire at night but he was his own shepherd and never very far from the scene of action.

"Ah've got a couple of cases for you today, Jim." His face, cracked and purpled by the weather, broke into a grin. "It's not really you ah need, it's that little lady's hand of yours and right sharpish, too."

He led the way to a bigger enclosure, holding several sheep. There was a scurry as we went in but he caught expertly at the fleece of a darting ewe. "This is the first one. You can see we haven't a deal o' time."

I lifted the woolly tail and gasped. The lamb's protruding head had swollen enormously to more than twice its size. The eyes were mere puffed slits and the tongue, blue and engorged, lolled from the mouth.

"Well I've seen a few big heads, Rob, but I think this takes the prize."

"Aye, the little beggar came with his legs back. Just beat me to it. Ah was only away for an hour but he was up like a football. By hell it doesn't take long. I know he wants his legs bringin' round, but what can I do with bloody great mitts like mine?" He held out his huge hands, rough and swollen with the years of work.

While he spoke I was stripping off my jacket and as I rolled my shirtsleeves high the wind struck like a knife at my shrinking flesh. I soaped my fingers quickly and began to feel for a space round the lamb's neck. For a moment the little eyes opened and regarded me disconsolately.

"He's alive, anyway," I said. "But he must feel terrible and he can't do a thing about it."

Easing my way round, I found a space down by the throat where I thought I might get through. This was where my "lady's hand" came in useful and I blessed it every spring; I could work inside the ewes with the minimum of discomfort to them and this was all-important because sheep, despite their outdoor hardiness, just won't stand rough treatment.

With the utmost care I inched my way along the curly wool of the neck to the shoulder. Another push forward and I was able to hook a finger round the leg and draw it forward until I could feel the flexure of the knee; a little more twiddling and I had hold of the tiny cloven foot and drew it gently out into the light of day.

Well that was half the job done. I got up from the sack where I was kneeling and went over to the bucket of warm water; I'd use my left hand for the other leg and began to soap it thoroughly while one of the ewes, marshaling her lambs around her, glared at me indignantly and gave a warning stamp of her foot.

Turning, I knelt again and began the same procedure and as I once more groped forward a tiny lamb dodged under my arm and began to suck at my patient's udder. He was clearly enjoying it, too, if the little tail, twirling inches from my face, meant anything.

"Where did this bloke come from?" I asked, still feeling round.

The farmer smiled. "Oh that's Herbert. Poor little youth's mother won't have 'im at any price. Took a spite at him at birth though she thinks world of her other lamb."

"Do you feed him, then?"

"Nay, I was going to put him with the pet lambs but I saw he was fendin' for himself. He pops from one ewe to t'other and gets a quick drink whenever he gets chance. I've never seen owt like it."

"Only a week old and an independent spirit, eh?"

"That's about the size of it, Jim. I notice 'is belly's full every mornin' so I reckon his ma must let him have a do during the night. She can't see him in the dark; it must be the look of him she can't stand."

I watched the little creature for a moment. To me he seemed as full of knock-kneed charm as any of the others. Sheep were funny things.

I soon had the other leg out and once that obstruction was removed the lamb followed easily. He was a grotesque sight lying on the strawed grass, his enormous head dwarfing his body, but his ribs were heaving reassuringly and I knew the head would shrink back to normal as quickly as it had expanded. I had another search round inside the ewe but the uterus was empty.

"There's no more, Rob," I said.

The farmer grunted. "Aye, I thowt so, just a big single 'un. They're the ones that cause the trouble."

Drying my arms, I watched Herbert. He had left my patient when she moved round to lick her lamb and he was moving speculatively among the other ewes. Some of them warned him off with a shake of the head but eventually he managed to sneak up on a big, wide-bodied sheep and pushed his head underneath her. Immediately she swung round and with a fierce upward butt of her hard skull she sent the little animal flying high in the air in a whirl of flailing legs. He landed with a thud on his back and as I hurried toward him he leaped to his feet and trotted away.

"Awd bitch!" shouted the farmer and as I turned to him in some concern he shrugged. "I know, poor little beggar, it's rough, but I've got a feelin' he wants it this way rather than being in the pen with the pet lambs. Look at 'im now."

Herbert, quite unabashed, was approaching another ewe and as she bent over her feeding trough he nipped underneath her and his tail went into action again. There was no doubt about it—that lamb had guts.

"Rob," I said as he caught my second patient, "why do you call him Herbert?"

"Well that's my youngest lad's name and that lamb's just like 'im the way he puts his head down and gets stuck in, fearless like."

I put my hand into the second ewe. Here was a glorious mix-up of three lambs; little heads, legs, a tail, all fighting their way toward the outside world and effectively stopping each other from moving an inch.

"She's been hanging about all morning and painin'," Rob said. "I knew summat was wrong."

Moving a hand carefully around inside I began the fascinating business of sorting out the tangle which is just about my favorite job in practice. I had to bring a head and two legs up together in order to deliver a lamb, but they had to belong to the same lamb or I was in trouble. It was a matter of tracing each leg back to see if it was hind or fore, to find if it joined the shoulder or disappeared into the depths.

After a few minutes I had a lamb assembled inside with his proper appendages but as I drew the legs into view the neck telescoped and the head slipped back; there was barely room for it to come through the pelvic bones along with the shoulders and I had to coax it through with a finger in the eye socket. This was groaningly painful as the bones squeezed my hand but only for a few seconds because the ewe gave a final strain and the little nose was visible. After that it was easy and I had him on the grass within seconds. The little creature gave a convulsive shake of his head and the farmer wiped him down quickly with straw before pushing him to his mother's head.

The ewe bent over him and began to lick his face and neck with little quick darts of her tongue; and she gave the deep chuckle of satisfaction that you hear from a sheep only at this time. The chuckling continued as I produced another pair of lambs from inside her, one of them hind end first and, toweling my arms again, I watched her nosing round her triplets delightedly.

Soon they began to answer her with wavering, high-pitched cries and as I drew my coat thankfully over my cold-reddened arms, lamb number one began to struggle to his knees. He couldn't quite make it to his feet and kept toppling onto his face but he knew where he was going all right; he was headed for that udder with a singleness of purpose which would soon be satisfied.

Despite the wind cutting over the straw bales into my face I found myself grinning down at the scene; this was always the best part, the wonder that was always fresh, the miracle you couldn't explain.

*   *   *

I heard from Rob Benson again a few days later. It was a Sunday afternoon and his voice was strained, almost panic-stricken.

"Jim, I've had a dog in among me in-lamb ewes. There was some folk up here with a car about dinner-time and my neighbor said they had an Alsatian and it was chasing the sheep all over the field. There's a hell of a mess—I tell you I'm frightened to look."

"I'm on my way." I dropped the receiver and hurried out to the car. I had a sinking dread of what would be waiting for me; the helpless animals lying with their throats torn, the terrifying lacerations of limbs and abdomen. I had seen it all before. The ones which didn't have to be slaughtered would need stitching and on the way I made a mental check of the stock of suture silk in the trunk.

The in-lamb ewes were in a field by the roadside and my heart gave a quick thump as I looked over the wall; arms resting on the rough loose stones, I gazed with sick dismay across the pasture. This was worse than I had feared. The long slope of turf was dotted with prostrate sheep—there must have been about fifty of them, motionless woolly mounds scattered at intervals on the green.

Rob was standing just inside the gate. He hardly looked at me. Just gestured with his head.

"Tell me what you think. I daren't go in there."

I left him and began to walk among the stricken creatures, rolling them over, lifting their legs, parting the fleece of their necks to examine them. Some were completely unconscious, others comatose; none of them could stand up. But as I worked my way up the field I felt a growing bewilderment. Finally I called back to the farmer.

"Rob, come over here. There's something very strange."

"Look," I said as the farmer approached hesitantly. "There's not a drop of blood nor a wound anywhere and yet all the sheep are flat out. I can't understand it."

Rob bent over and gently raised a lolling head. "Aye, you're right. What the 'ell's done it, then?"

At the moment I couldn't answer him, but a little bell was tinkling far away in the back of my mind. There was something familiar about that ewe the farmer had just handled. She was one of the few able to support herself on her chest and she was lying there, blank-eyed and oblivious of everything; but . . . that drunken nodding of the head, that watery nasal discharge . . . I had seen it before. I knelt down and as I put my face close to hers I heard a faint bubbling—almost a rattling—in her breathing. I knew then.

"It's calcium deficiency," I cried and began to gallop down the slope toward the car.

Rob trotted alongside me. "But what the 'ell?

They get that *after* lambin', don't they?"

"Yes, usually," I puffed, "but sudden exertion and stress can bring it on."

"Well ah never knew that," panted Rob. "How does it happen?"

I saved my breath. I wasn't going to start an exposition on the effects of sudden derangement of the parathyroid. I was more concerned with wondering if I had enough calcium in the trunk for fifty ewes. It was reassuring to see the long row of round tin caps peeping from their cardboard box; I must have filled up recently.

I injected the first ewe in the vein just to check my diagnosis—calcium works as quickly as that in sheep, and felt a quiet elation as the unconscious animal began to blink and tremble, then tried to struggle onto its chest.

"We'll inject the others under the skin," I said. "It'll save time."

I began to work my way up the field. Rob pulled forward the fore leg of each sheep so that I could insert the needle under the convenient patch of unwoolled skin just behind the elbow, and by the time I was halfway up the slope the ones at the bottom were walking about and getting their heads into the food troughs and hayracks.

It was one of the most satisfying experiences of my working life. Not clever, but a magical transfiguration;

from despair to hope, from death to life within minutes.

I was throwing the empty bottles into the trunk when Rob spoke. He was looking wonderingly up at the last of the ewes getting to its feet at the far end of the field.

"Well Jim, I'll tell you. I've never seen owt like that afore. But there's one thing bothers me." He turned to me and his weathered features screwed up in puzzlement. "Ah can understand how gettin' chased by a dog could affect some of them ewes, but why should the whole bloody lot go down?"

"Rob," I said. "I don't know."

And, thirty years later, I still wonder. I still don't know why the whole bloody lot went down.

I thought Rob had enough to worry about at the time, so I didn't point out to him that other complications could be expected after the Alsatian episode. I wasn't surprised when I had a call to the Benson farm within days.

I met him again on the hillside with the same wind whipping over the straw bale pens. The lambs had been arriving in a torrent and the noise was louder than ever. He led me to my patient.

"There's one with a bellyful of dead lambs, I reckon," he said, pointing to a ewe with her head drooping, ribs heaving. She stood quite motionless and made no attempt to move away when I went up to her; this one was really sick and as the stink of decomposition came up to me I knew the farmer's diagnosis was right.

"Well I suppose it had to happen to one at least after that chasing round," I said. "Let's see what we can do, anyway."

This kind of lambing is without charm but it has to be done to save the ewe. I delivered the little bodies with least discomfort to the mother. When I had finished, the ewe's head was almost touching the ground; she was panting rapidly and grating her teeth. I had nothing to offer her—no wriggling new creature for her to lick and revive her interest in life. What she needed was an injection of penicillin, but this was 1939 and the antibiotics were still a little way round the corner.

"Well I wouldn't give much for her," Rob grunted. "Is there owt more you can do?"

"Oh, I'll give her an injection, but what she needs most is a lamb to look after. You know as well as I do that ewes in this condition usually give up if they've nothing to occupy them. You haven't a spare lamb to put on her, have you?"

"Not right now, I haven't. And it's now she needs it. Tomorrow'll be too late."

Just at that moment a familiar figure wandered into view. It was Herbert, the unwanted lamb, easily recognizable as he prowled from sheep to sheep in search of nourishment.

"Hey, do you think she'd take that little chap?" I asked the farmer.

He looked doubtful. "Well I don't know; he's a bit old. Nearly a fortnight and they like 'em newly born."

"But it's worth a try, isn't it? Why not try the old trick on her?"

Rob grinned. "Okay, we'll do that. There's nowt to lose. Anyway the little youth isn't much bigger than a newborn 'un. He hasn't grown as fast as his mates." He took out his penknife and quickly skinned one of the dead lambs, then he tied the skin over Herbert's back and round his jutting ribs.

"Poor little beggar, there's nowt on 'im," he muttered. "If this doesn't work he's going in with the pet lambs."

When he had finished he set Herbert on the grass and the lamb, resolute little character that he was, bored straight in under the sick ewe and began to suck. It seemed he wasn't having much success because he gave the udder a few peremptory thumps with his hard little head; then his tail began to wiggle.

"She's lettin' him have a drop, any road," Rob laughed.

Herbert was a type you couldn't ignore and the big sheep, sick as she was, just had to turn her head for a look at him. She sniffed along the tied-on skin in a noncommittal way then after a few seconds she gave a few quick licks and the merest beginning of the familiar deep chuckle.

I began to gather up my gear. "I hope he makes it," I said. "Those two need each other." As I left the pen Herbert, in his new jacket, was still working away.

For the next week I hardly seemed to have my coat on. The flood of sheep work was at its peak and I spent hours of every day with my arms in and out of buckets of hot water in all corners of the district; in the pens, in dark nooks in farm buildings or very often in the open fields, because the farmers of those days didn't find anything disturbing in the sight of a vet kneeling in his shirtsleeves for an hour in the rain.

I had one more visit to Rob Benson's place, to a ewe with a prolapsed uterus after lambing.

Afterward, the ewe trotted away unperturbed with her family to join the rapidly growing flock whose din was all around us.

"Look!" Rob cried. "There's that awd ewe with Herbert. Over there on t'right—in the middle of that bunch." They all looked the same to me but to Rob, like all shepherds, they were as different as people and he picked out these two effortlessly.

They were near the top of the field and as I wanted to have a close look at them we maneuvered them into a corner. The ewe, fiercely possessive, stamped her foot at us as we approached, and Herbert, who had discarded his woolly jacket, held close to the flank of his new mother. He was, I noticed, faintly obese in appearance.

"You couldn't call him a runt now, Rob," I said.

The farmer laughed. "Nay, t'awd lass has a bag like a cow and Herbert's gettin' the lot. By gaw, he's in clover is that little youth and I reckon he saved the ewe's life—she'd have pegged out all right, but she never looked back once he came along."

I looked away, over the noisy pens, over the hundreds of sheep moving across the fields. I turned to the farmer. "I'm afraid you've seen a lot of me lately, Rob. I hope this is the last visit."

"Aye well it could be. We're getting well through now . . . but it's a 'ell of a time, lambin', isn't it?"

"It is that. Well I must be off—I'll leave you to it." I turned and made my way down the hillside, my arms raw and chafing in my sleeves, my cheeks whipped by the eternal wind gusting over the grass. At the gate I stopped and gazed back at the wide landscape, ribbed and streaked by the last of the winter's snow, and at the dark gray banks of cloud riding across on the wind followed by lakes of brightest blue; and in seconds the fields and walls and woods burst into vivid life and I had to close my eyes against the sun's glare. As I stood there the distant uproar came faintly down to me, the tumultuous harmony from deepest bass to highest treble; demanding, anxious, angry, loving.

The sound of sheep, the sound of spring.

A Lesson from the Horse's Mouth

Probably the most dramatic occurrence in the history of veterinary practice was the disappearance of the draft horse. It is an almost incredible fact that this glory and mainstay of the profession just melted quietly away within a few years. And I was one of those who was there to see it happen.

When I first came to Darrowby the tractor had already begun to take over, but tradition dies hard in the agricultural world and there were still a lot of horses around. Although my veterinary education had been geared to things equine with everything else a poor second, I have to admit that I was not, am not, and never will be a true horseman. It is difficult to define the terms but I am convinced that horsemen are either born or acquire the talent in early childhood. I have the ability to treat sick horses efficiently, and I have great admiration for them, but the power the real horseman has to soothe and quieten such an animal is beyond my reach. Thinking back over my life, I wondered if there was an occasion which might have affected my attitude toward the horse. And then I remembered.

I was back in Scotland, I was seventeen and I was walking under the arch of the Veterinary College into Montrose Street. I had been a student for three days but not until this afternoon had I felt the thrill of fulfillment. Messing about with botany and zoology was all right but this afternoon had been the real thing; I had had my first lecture in animal husbandry.

The subject had been the points of the horse. Professor Grant had hung up a life-size picture of a horse and gone over it from nose to tail, indicating the withers, the stifle, the hock, the poll and all the other rich, equine terms. And the professor had been wise; to make his lecture more interesting he kept throwing in little practical points like, "This is where we find curb," or "Here is the site for windgalls." He talked of thoroughpins and sidebones, splints and quittor; things the students wouldn't learn about for another four years, but it brought it all to life.

The words were still spinning in my head as I walked slowly down the sloping street. This was what

I had come for. I felt as though I had undergone an initiation and become a member of an exclusive club. I really knew about horses. And I was wearing a brand-new riding coat with all sorts of extra straps and buckles which slapped against my legs as I turned the corner of the hill into busy Newton Road.

I could hardly believe my luck when I saw the horse. It was standing outside the library below Queen's Cross like something left over from another age. It drooped dispiritedly between the shafts of a coal cart which stood like an island in an eddying stream of cars and buses. Pedestrians hurried by, uncaring, but I had the feeling that fortune was smiling on me.

A horse. Not just a picture but a real, genuine

horse. Stray words from the lecture floated up into my mind; the pastern, cannon bone, coronet and all those markings; snip, blaze, white sock near hind. I stood on the pavement and examined the animal critically.

I thought it must be obvious to every passerby that here was a true expert. Not just an inquisitive onlooker but a man who knew and understood all. I felt clothed in a visible aura of horsiness. I took a few steps up and down, hands deep in the pockets of the new riding coat, eyes probing for possible shoeing faults or curbs or bog spavins. So thorough was my inspection that I worked round to the off side of the horse and stood perilously among the racing traffic.

I glanced around at the people hurrying past. Nobody seemed to care, not even the horse. He was a large one, at least seventeen hands, and he gazed apathetically down the street, easing his hind legs alternately in a bored manner. I hated to leave him but I had completed my examination and it was time I was on my way. But I felt that I ought to make a gesture before I left; something to communicate to the horse that I understood his problems and that we belonged to the same brotherhood. I stepped briskly forward and patted him on the neck.

Quick as a striking snake, the horse whipped downward and seized my shoulder in his great strong teeth. He laid back his ears, rolled his eyes wickedly and hoisted me up, almost off my feet. I hung there helplessly, suspended like a lopsided puppet. I wriggled and kicked but the teeth were clamped immovably in the material of my coat.

There was no doubt about the interest of the passersby now. The grotesque sight of a man hanging from a horse's mouth brought them to a sudden halt and a crowd formed with people looking over each other's shoulders and others fighting at the back to see what was going on.

A horrified old lady was crying, "Oh, poor boy! Help him, somebody!" Some of the braver characters tried pulling at me but the horse whickered ominously and hung on tighter. Conflicting advice was shouted from all sides. With deep shame I saw two attractive girls in the front row giggling helplessly.

Appalled at the absurdity of my position, I began to thrash about wildly; my shirt collar tightened round my throat; a stream of the horse's saliva trickled down the front of my coat. I could feel myself choking and was giving up hope when a man pushed his way through the crowd.

He was very small. Angry eyes glared from a face blackened by coal dust. Two empty sacks were draped over an arm.

"Whit the 'ell's this?" he shouted. A dozen replies babbled in the air.

"Can ye no leave the bloody hoarse alone?" he yelled into my face. I made no reply, being pop-eyed, half throttled and in no mood for conversation.

The coalman turned his fury on the horse. "Drop him, ya big bastard! Go on, let go, drop him!"

Getting no response he dug the animal viciously in the belly with his thumb. The horse took the point at once and released me like an obedient dog dropping a bone. I fell on my knees and ruminated in the gutter for a while until I could breathe more easily. As from a great distance I could still hear the little man shouting at me.

After some time I stood up. The coalman was still shouting and the crowd was listening appreciatively. "Whit d'ye think you're playing at—keep yer hands off ma bloody hoarse—get the poliss tae ye."

I looked down at my new coat. The shoulder was chewed to a sodden mass. I felt I must escape and began to edge my way through the crowd. Some of the faces were concerned but most were grinning. Once clear I started to walk away rapidly and as I turned the corner the last faint cry from the coalman reached me.

"Dinna meddle wi' things ye ken nuthin' aboot!"

Tricki Woo
Requests the Pleasure

I flipped idly through the morning mail. The usual stack of bills, circulars, brightly colored advertisements for new drugs; after a few months the novelty had worn off and I hardly bothered to read them. I had almost reached the bottom of the pile when I came on something different; an expensive-looking envelope in heavy, deckle-edged paper addressed to me personally. I ripped it open and pulled out a gilt-bordered card which I scanned quickly. I felt my face redden as I slipped the card into an inside pocket.

My partner, Siegfried, finished ticking off the visits and looked up. "What are you looking so guilty about, James? Your past catching up with you? What is it, anyway—a letter from an outraged mother?"

"Go on then," I said sheepishly, pulling out the

card and handing it to him, "have a good laugh. I suppose you'd find out, anyway."

Siegfried's face was expressionless as he read the card aloud. "Tricki requests the pleasure of Uncle Herriot's company on Friday, February fifth. Drinks and dancing." He looked up and spoke seriously. "Now isn't that nice? You know, that must be one of the most generous Pekingeses in England. Sending you kippers and tomatoes and hampers isn't enough—he has to ask you to his home for a party."

I grabbed the card and slipped it out of sight. "All right, all right, I know. But what am I supposed to do?"

"Do? What you do is to sit down right away and get a letter off saying thank you very much, you'll be there on February the fifth. Mrs. Pumphrey's parties are famous. Mountains of exotic food, rivers of champagne. Don't miss it whatever you do."

"Will there be a lot of people there?" I asked, shuffling my feet.

Siegfried struck himself on the forehead with his open hand. "Of course there'll be a lot of people. What d'you think? Did you expect it would be just you and Tricki? You'd have a few beers together and then you'd dance a slow foxtrot with him? The cream of the county will be there in full regalia but my guess is that there will be no more honored guest than Uncle

Herriot. Why? Because Mrs. Pumphrey invited the others but Tricki invited you."

"Okay, okay," I groaned. "I'll be on my own and I haven't got a proper evening suit. I don't fancy it."

Siegfried rose and put a hand on my shoulder. "My dear chap, don't mess about. Sit down and accept the invitation and then go into Brawton and hire a suit for the night. You won't be on your own for long—the debs will be tramping over each other for a dance with you." He gave the shoulder a final pat before walking to the door. Before leaving he turned round and his expression was grave. "And remember for Pete's sake don't write to Mrs. Pumphrey. Address your letter to Tricki himself or you're sunk."

I had a lot of mixed feelings churning around in me when I presented myself at the Pumphrey home on the night of February 5. A maid led me into the hall and I could see Mrs. Pumphrey at the entrance to the ballroom receiving her guests and, beyond, an elegant throng standing around with drinks. There was a well-bred clamor, a general atmosphere of wealth. I straightened the tie on my hired outfit, took a deep breath and waited.

Mrs. Pumphrey was smiling sweetly as she shook hands with the couple in front of me but when she saw me her face became radiant. "Oh Mr. Herriot, how nice of you to come. Tricki was so delighted to have your letter—in fact, we really must go in and see him now." She led me across the hall.

"He's in the morning room," she whispered. "Between ourselves he finds these affairs rather a bore, but he'll be simply furious if I don't take you in for a moment."

Tricki was curled up in an armchair by the side of a bright fire. When he saw me he jumped on the back of the chair barking in delight, his huge, laughing mouth bisecting his face. I was trying to fend off his attempts to lick my face when I caught sight of two large food bowls on the carpet. One contained about a pound of chopped chicken, the other a mass of crumbled cake.

"Mrs. Pumphrey!" I thundered, pointing at the bowls. The poor woman put her hand to her mouth and shrank away from me.

"Oh do forgive me," she wailed, her face a picture of guilt. "It's just a special treat because he's alone tonight. And the weather is so cold, too." She clasped her hands and looked at me abjectly.

"I'll forgive you," I said sternly, "if you will remove half the chicken and *all* the cake."

Fluttering, like a little girl caught in naughtiness, she did as I said.

I parted regretfully from the little Peke. It had been a busy day and I was sleepy from the hours in the biting cold. This room with its fire and soft lighting looked more inviting than the noisy glitter of the ball-room and I would have preferred to curl up here with Tricki on my knee for an hour or two.

Mrs. Pumphrey became brisk. "Now you must come and meet some of my friends." We went into the ballroom where light blazed down from three cut-glass chandeliers and was reflected dazzlingly down from the cream and gold many-mirrored walls. We moved from group to group as Mrs. Pumphrey intro-duced me and I squirmed in embarrassment as I heard myself described as "Tricki's dear kind uncle." But either they were people of superb self-control or they were familiar with their hostess's blind spot because the information was received with complete gravity.

Along one wall a five-piece orchestra was tuning up; white-jacketed waiters hurried among the guests with trays of food and drinks. Mrs. Pumphrey stopped one of the waiters. "François, some cham-pagne for this gentleman."

"Yes, Madame." The waiter proffered his tray.

"No, no, no, not those. One of the big glasses."

François hurried away and returned with some-thing like a soup plate with a stem. It was brimming with champagne.

"François."

"Yes, Madame?"

"This is Mr. Herriot. I want you to take a good look at him."

The waiter turned a pair of sad spaniel eyes on me and drank me in for a few moments.

"I want you to look after him. See that his glass is full and that he has plenty to eat."

"Certainly, Madame." He bowed and moved away.

I buried my face in the ice-cold champagne and when I looked up, there was François holding out a tray of smoked salmon sandwiches.

It was like that all the evening. François seemed always to be at my elbow, filling up the enormous glass or pushing dainties at me. I found it delightful; the salty snacks brought on a thirst which I quenched with deep drafts of champagne, then I had more snacks which made me thirsty again and Fran-çois would unfailingly pop up with the magnum.

It was the first time I had had the opportunity of drinking champagne by the pint and it was a rewarding experience. I was quickly aware of a glorious lightness, a heightening of the perceptions. I stopped being overawed by this new world and began to enjoy it. I danced with everybody in sight—sleek young beauties, elderly dowagers and twice with a giggling Mrs. Pumphrey.

Or I just talked. And it was witty talk; I repeatedly amazed myself by my lightning shafts. Once I caught sight of myself in a mirror—a distinguished figure, glass in hand, the hired suit hanging on me with quiet grace. It took my breath away.

Eating, drinking, talking, dancing, the evening winged past. When it was time to go and I had my coat on and was shaking hands with Mrs. Pumphrey in the hall, François appeared again with a bowl of hot soup. He seemed to be worried lest I grow faint on the journey home.

After the soup, Mrs. Pumphrey said, "And now you must come and say good-night to Tricki. He'll never forgive you if you don't." We went into his room and the little dog yawned from the depths of the chair and wagged his tail. Mrs. Pumphrey put her hand on my sleeve. "While you're here, I wonder if you would be so kind as to examine his claws. I've been so worried in case they might be growing too long."

I lifted up the paws one by one and scrutinized the claws while Tricki lazily licked my hands. "No, you needn't worry, they're perfectly all right."

"Thank you so much, I'm so grateful to you. Now you must wash your hands."

In the familiar bathroom with the sea-green basins

and the enameled fishes on the walls and the dressing table and the bottles on the glass shelves, I looked around as the steaming water ran from the tap. There was my own towel by the basin and the usual new slab of soap—soap that lathered in an instant and gave off an expensive scent. It was the final touch of balm on a gracious evening. It had been a few hours of luxury and light and I carried the memory back with me to Skeldale House.

I got into bed, switched off the light and lay on my back looking up into the darkness. Snatches of music still tinkled about in my head and I was beginning to swim back to the ballroom when the phone rang.

"This is Atkinson of Beck Cottage," a faraway voice said. "I 'ave a sow 'ere what can't get pigged. She's been on all night. Will you come?"

I looked at the clock as I put down the receiver. It was 2 A.M. I felt numbed. A farrowing right on top of the champagne and the smoked salmon and those little biscuits with the black heaps of caviar. And at Beck Cottage, one of the most primitive small holdings in the district. It wasn't fair.

Sleepily, I took off my pajamas and pulled on my shirt. As I reached for the stiff, worn corduroys I used for work, I tried not to look at the hired suit hanging on a corner of the wardrobe.

I groped my way down the long garden to the

garage. In the darkness of the yard I closed my eyes and the great chandeliers blazed again, the mirrors flashed and the music played.

It was only two miles out to Beck Cottage. It lay in a hollow and in the winter the place was a sea of mud. I left my card and squelched through the blackness to the door of the house. My knock was unanswered and I moved across to the cluster of buildings opposite and opened the half-door into the byre. The warm, sweet bovine smell met me as I peered toward a light show-ing dimly at the far end where a figure was standing.

I went inside past the shadowy row of cows stand-ing side by side with broken wooden partitions between them and past the mounds of manure piled behind them. Mr. Atkinson didn't believe in mucking out too often.

Stumbling over the uneven floor, I arrived at the end where a pen had been made by closing off a corner with a gate. I could just make out the form of a pig, pale in the gloom, lying on her side. There was a scanty bed of straw under her and she lay very still except for the trembling of her flanks. As I watched, she caught her breath and strained for a few seconds, stopped, then the straining began again.

Mr. Atkinson received me without enthusiasm. He was middle-aged, sported a week's growth of beard and wore an ancient hat with a brim which flopped round his ears. He stood hunched against a wall, one hand deep in a ragged pocket, the other holding a bicycle lamp with a fast-failing battery.

"Is this all the light we've got?" I asked.

"Aye, it is," Mr. Atkinson replied, obviously surprised. He looked from the lamp to me with a "what more does he want?" expression.

"Let's have it, then." I trained the feeble beam on my patient.

"Just a young pig, isn't she?"

"Aye, nobbut a gilt. Fust litter."

The pig strained again, shuddered and lay still.

"Something stuck there, I reckon," I said. "Will you bring me a bucket of hot water, some soap and a towel, please?"

"Haven't got no 'ot water. Fire's out."

"Okay, bring me whatever you've got."

The farmer clattered away down the byre taking the light with him and, with the darkness, the music came back again. It was a Strauss waltz and I was dancing with Lady Frenswick; she was young and very fair and she laughed as I swung her round. I could see her white shoulders and the diamonds winking at her throat and the wheeling mirrors.

Mr. Atkinson came shuffling back and dumped a bucket of water on the floor. I dipped a finger in the water; it was ice cold. And the bucket had seen many hard years—I would have to watch my arms on the jagged rim.

Quickly stripping off jacket and shirt, I sucked in my breath as a villainous draft blew through a crack onto my back.

"Soap, please," I said through clenched teeth.

"In t'bucket."

I plunged an arm into the water, shivered, and felt my way round until I found a roundish object about the size of a golf ball. I pulled it out and examined it; it was hard and smooth and speckled like a pebble from the seashore and, optimistically, I began to rub it between my hands and up my arms, waiting for the lather to form. But the soap was impervious; it yielded nothing.

I discarded the idea of asking for another piece in case this would be construed as another complaint. Instead, I borrowed the light and tracked down the byre into the yard, the mud sucking at my boots, goose pimples rearing on my chest. I searched around in the trunk, listening to my teeth chattering, until I came on a jar of antiseptic lubricating cream.

Back in the pen, I smeared the cream on my arm, knelt behind the pig and gently inserted my hand inside her. I was forced to roll over on my side. The stones were cold and wet but I forgot my discomfort when my fingers touched something; it was a tiny tail. Almost a transverse presentation, biggish piglet stuck like a cork in a bottle.

Using one finger, I worked the hind legs back until I was able to grasp them and draw the piglet out. "This is the one that's been causing the trouble. He's dead, I'm afraid—been squashed in there too long. But there could be some live ones still inside. I'll have another feel."

I greased my arm and got down again. Almost at arm's length, I found another piglet and I was feeling at the face when a set of minute but very sharp teeth sank into my finger.

I yelped and looked up at the farmer from my stony bed. "This one's alive, anyway. I'll soon have him out."

But the piglet had other ideas. He showed no desire to leave his warm haven and every time I got hold of his slippery little foot between my fingers he jerked it away. After a minute or two of this game I felt a cramping in my arm. I relaxed and lay back, my head resting on the cobbles, my arm still inside the pig. I closed my eyes and immediately I was back in the ballroom, in the warmth and the brilliant light. I was holding out my immense glass while François poured from the magnum; then I was dancing, close to the orchestra this time and the leader, beating time with one hand, turned round and smiled into my face; smiled and bowed as though he had been looking for me all his life.

I smiled back but the bandleader's face dissolved and there was only Mr. Atkinson looking down at me expressionlessly, his unshaven jaw and shaggy eyebrows thrown into sinister relief by the light striking up from the bicycle lamp.

I shook myself and raised my cheek from the floor. This wouldn't do. Falling asleep on the job; either I was very tired or there was still some champagne in me. I reached again and grasped the foot firmly between two fingers and this time, despite his struggles, the piglet was hauled out into the world. Once arrived, he seemed to accept the situation and tottered round philosophically to his mother's udder.

"She's not helping at all," I said. "Been on so long that she's exhausted. I'm going to give her an injection."

Another numbing expedition through the mud to the car, a shot of pituitrin into the gilt's thigh and within minutes the action began with powerful con-

tractions of the uterus. There was no obstruction now and soon a wriggling pink piglet was deposited in the straw; then quite quickly another and another.

"Coming off the assembly line now, all right," I said. Mr. Atkinson grunted.

Eight piglets were born and the light from the lamp was almost giving out.

I rubbed my cold arms. "Well, I should say that's the lot now." I felt suddenly chilled; I couldn't say how long I had been standing there looking at the wonder that never grew stale; the little pigs struggling onto their legs and making their way unguided to the long double row of teats; the mother with her first family easing herself over to expose as much as possible of her udder to the hungry mouths.

Better get dressed quickly. I had another try at the marblelike soap but it defeated me as easily as the first time. I wondered how long it had been in the family. Down my right side my cheek and ribs were caked with dirt and mucus. I did my best to scrape some off with my fingernails, then I swilled myself down with the cold water from the bucket.

"Have you a towel there?" I gasped.

Mr. Atkinson wordlessly handed me a sack. Its edges were stiff with old manure and it smelled musty from the meal it had long since contained. I took it and began to rub my chest and as the sour grains of the meal powdered my skin, the last bubbles of champagne left me, drifted up through the gaps in the tiles and burst sadly in the darkness beyond.

I dragged my shirt over my gritty back, feeling a sense of coming back to my own world. I buttoned my coat, picked up the syringe and the bottle of pituitrin and climbed out of the pen. I had a last look before I left. The bicycle lamp was shedding its final faint glow and I had to lean over the gate to see the row of little pigs sucking busily, utterly absorbed. The gilt carefully shifted her position and grunted. It was a grunt of deep content.

Yes, I was back and it was all right. I drove

through the mud and up the hill where I had to get out to open a gate and the wind, with the cold, clean smell of the frosty grass in it, caught at my face. I stood for a while looking across the dark fields, thinking of the night which was ending now. My mind went back to my school days and an old gentleman talking to the class about careers. He had said: "If you decide to become a veterinary surgeon you will never grow rich but you will have a life of endless interest and variety."

I laughed aloud in the darkness and as I got into the car I was still chuckling. That old chap certainly wasn't kidding. Variety. That was it—variety.

Susie, Messenger of Love

The big room at Skeldale House was full. It seemed to me that this room with its graceful alcoves, high carved ceilings and french windows lay at the center of our life in Darrowby. It was where Siegfried, his brother Tristan, and I gathered when the day's work was done, toasting our feet by the white wood fireplace with the glass-fronted cupboard on top, talking over the day's events. It was the heart of our bachelor existence, sitting there in a happy stupor, reading, listening to the radio, Tristan usually flipping effortlessly through the *Daily Telegraph* crossword.

It was where Siegfried entertained his friends and there was a constant stream of them—old and young, male and female. But tonight it was Tristan's turn and the pack of young people with drinks in their hands were there at his invitation. And they wouldn't need much persuasion. Though just about the opposite of his brother in many ways he had the same attractiveness which brought the friends running at the crook of a finger.

The occasion was the Daffodil Ball at the Drovers' Arms and we were dressed in our best. This was a different kind of function from the usual village institute hop with the farm lads in their big boots and music from a scraping fiddle and piano. It was a proper dance with a popular local band—Lenny Butterfield and his Hot Shots—and was an annual affair to herald the arrival of spring.

When we arrived at the Drovers' the bar was congested while only a dedicated few circled round the ballroom. But as time went on more and more couples ventured out and by ten o'clock the dance floor was truly packed and I soon found I was enjoying myself. Tristan's friends were an effervescent bunch; likable young men and attractive girls; I just couldn't help having a good time.

There was no pairing off in our party and I danced with all the girls in turn. At the peak of the evening I was jockeying my way around the floor with Daphne and the way she was constructed made it a rewarding experience. I never have been one for skinny women but I suppose you could say that Daphne's development had strayed a little too far in the other direction. She wasn't fat, just lavishly endowed.

Battling through the crush, colliding with exuberant neighbors, bouncing deliciously off Daphne, with everybody singing as they danced and the Hot Shots pouring out an insistent boom-boom beat, I felt I hadn't a care in the world. And then, across the dance floor, I saw Helen.

When the music stopped I returned Daphne to her friends and went to find Tristan. The comfortable little bar in the Drovers' was overflowing and the temperature like an oven. Through an almost impenetrable fog of cigarette smoke I discerned my colleague on a high stool holding court with a group of perspiring revelers. Tristan himself looked cool and, as always, profoundly content. He drained his glass, smacked his lips gently as though it had been the best pint of beer he'd ever tasted, then, as he reached across the counter and courteously requested a refill, he spotted me struggling toward him.

When I reached his stool he laid an affable hand on my shoulder. "Ah, Jim, nice to see you. Splendid dance, this, don't you think?"

I didn't bring up the fact that I hadn't seen him on the floor yet, but making my voice casual I mentioned that Helen was there.

Tristan nodded benignly.

"Yes, saw her come in. Why don't you go and dance with her?"

"I can't do that. She's with a partner—young Edmundson."

"Not at all." Tristan surveyed his fresh pint with a critical eye and took an exploratory sip. "She's with a party, like us. No partner."

"How do you know that?"

"I watched all the fellows hand their coats out there while the girls went upstairs. No reason at all why you shouldn't have a dance with her."

"I see." I hesitated for a few moments, then made my way back to the ballroom.

But it wasn't as easy as that. I had to keep doing my duty with the girls in our group and whenever I headed for Helen she was whisked away by one of her men friends before I got near her. At times I fancied she was looking over at me but I couldn't be sure; the only thing I knew for certain was that I wasn't enjoying myself anymore; the magic and gaiety had gone and I felt a rising misery at the thought that this was going to be another of my frustrating contacts with Helen when all I could do was look at her hopelessly. Only this time was worse—I hadn't even spoken to her.

I was almost relieved when the manager came up and told me there was a call for me. I went to the phone and spoke to Mrs. Hall, our housekeeper at Skeldale House. There was a bitch in trouble whelping and I had to go. I looked at my watch—after midnight, so that was the end of the dance for me.

I stood for a moment listening to the muffled thudding from the dance floor, then slowly pulled on my coat before going in to say good-bye to Tristan's friends. I exchanged a few words with them, waved, then turned back and pushed the swing door open.

Helen was standing there, about a foot away from me. Her hand was on the door, too. I didn't wonder whether she was going in or out but stared dumbly into her smiling blue eyes.

"Leaving already, Jim?" she said.

"Yes, I've got a call, I'm afraid."

"Oh what a shame. I hope it's nothing very serious."

I opened my mouth to speak, but her dark beauty and the very nearness of her suddenly filled my world and a wave of hopeless longing swept over and submerged me. I slid my hand a few inches down the door and gripped hers as a drowning man might and wonderingly I felt her fingers come round and entwine themselves tightly in mine.

And in an instant there was no band, no noise, no people, just the two of us standing, very close in the doorway.

"Come with me," I said.

Helen's eyes were very large as she smiled that smile I knew so well.

"I'll get my coat," she murmured.

This wasn't really me, I thought, standing on the hall carpet watching Helen trotting quickly up the stairs, but I had to believe it as she reappeared on the landing pulling on her coat. Outside, on the cobbles of the marketplace, my car, too, appeared to be taken by surprise because it roared into life at the first touch of the starter.

I had to go back to the surgery for my whelping instruments and in the silent moonlit street we got out and I opened the big white door to Skeldale House.

And once in the passage it was the most natural thing in the world to take her in my arms and kiss her gratefully and unhurriedly. I had waited a long time for this and the minutes flowed past unnoticed as we stood there, our feet on the black and red eighteenth-century tiles, our heads almost touching the vast picture of the Death of Nelson which dominated the entrance.

We kissed again at the first bend of the passage under the companion picture of the Meeting of Wellington and Blücher at Waterloo. We kissed at the second bend by the tall cupboard where Siegfried kept his riding coats and boots. We kissed in the dispensary in between searching for my instruments. Then we tried it out in the garden and this was the best of all, with the flowers still and expectant in the moonlight and the fragrance of the moist earth and grass rising about us.

I have never driven so slowly to a case. About ten miles an hour with Helen's head on my shoulder and all the scents of spring drifting in through the open window. And it was like sailing from stormy seas into a sweet, safe harbor, like coming home.

The light in the cottage window was the only one showing in the sleeping village and when I knocked at the door Bert Chapman answered. Bert was a council roadman—one of the breed for whom I felt an abiding affinity. The councilmen were my brethren of the roads. Like me they spent most of their lives on the lonely byways around Darrowby and I saw them most days of the week, repairing the tarmac, cutting back the grass verges in the summer, gritting and snow plowing in the winter.

I had seen Bert Chapman just a day or two ago, sitting on a grassy bank, his shovel by his side, a vast sandwich in his hand. He had raised a corded forearm in salute, a broad smile bisecting his round, sun-reddened face. He had looked eternally carefree but tonight his smile was strained.

"I'm sorry to bother you this late, Mr. Herriot," he said as he ushered us into the house, "but I'm gettin' a bit worried about Susie. Her pups are due and she's been making a bed for them and messing about all day but nowt's happened. I was goin' to leave her till morning but about midnight she started panting like 'ell—I don't like the look of her."

Susie was one of my regular patients. Her big, burly master was always bringing her to the surgery, a little shamefaced at his solicitude, and when I saw him sitting in the waiting room looking strangely out of place among the ladies with their pets, he usually said, "T'missus asked me to bring Susie." But it was a transparent excuse.

"She's nobbut a little mongrel, but very faithful," Bert said, still apologetic, but I could understand how he felt about Susie, a shaggy little ragamuffin whose only wile was to put her paws on my knees and laugh up into my face with her tail lashing. I found her irresistible.

But she was a very different character tonight. As we went into the living room of the cottage the little animal crept from her basket, gave a single indeterminate wag of her tail, then stood miserably in the middle of the floor, her ribs heaving. As I bent to examine her she turned a wide, panting mouth and anxious eyes up to me.

I ran my hands over her abdomen. I don't think I have ever felt a more bloated little dog; she was as round as a football, absolutely bulging with pups, ready to pop, but nothing was happening.

"What do you think?" Bert's face was haggard under his sunburn and he touched the dog's head briefly with a big calloused hand.

"I don't know yet, Bert," I said. "I'll have to have a feel inside. Bring me some hot water, will you?"

I added some antiseptic to the water, soaped my hand and with one finger carefully explored inside.

There was a pup there, all right; my fingertip brushed across the nostrils, the tiny mouth and tongue, but he was jammed in that passage like a cork in a bottle.

Squatting back on my heels I turned to the Chapmans. "I'm afraid there's a big pup stuck fast. I have a feeling that if she could get rid of this chap the others would come away. They'd probably be smaller."

"Is there any way of shiftin' him, Mr. Herriot?" Bert asked.

I paused for a moment. "I'm going to put forceps on his head and see if he'll move. I don't like using forceps but I'm going to have one careful try and if it doesn't work I'll have to take her back to the surgery for a caesarean."

"An operation?" Bert said hollowly. He gulped and glanced fearfully at his wife. Like many big men he had married a tiny woman and at this moment Mrs. Chapman looked even smaller than her four feet eleven inches as she huddled in her chair and stared at me with wide eyes.

"Oh I wish we'd never had her mated," she wailed, wringing her hands. "I told Bert five year old was too late for a first litter but he wouldn't listen. And now we're maybe going to lose 'er."

I hastened to reassure her. "No, she isn't too old, and everything may be all right. Let's just see how we get on."

I boiled the instrument for a few minutes on the

stove, then kneeled behind my patient again. I poised the forceps for a moment and at the flash of steel a gray tinge crept under Bert's sunburn and his wife coiled herself into a ball in her chair. Obviously they were nonstarters as assistants so Helen held Susie's head while I once more reached in toward the pup. There was desperately little room but I managed to direct the forceps along my finger until they touched the nose. Then very gingerly I opened the jaws and pushed them forward with the very gentlest pressure until I was able to clamp them on either side of the head.

I'd soon know now. In a situation like this you can't do any pulling, you can only try to ease the thing along. This I did and I fancied I felt just a bit of movement. I tried again and there was no doubt about it, the pup was coming toward me. Susie, too, appeared to sense that things were taking a turn for the better. She cast off her apathy and began to strain lustily.

It was no trouble after that and I was able to draw the pup forth almost without resistance.

"I'm afraid this one'll be dead," I said, and as the tiny creature lay across my palm there was no sign of breathing. But pinching the chest between thumb and forefinger I could feel the heart pulsing steadily and I quickly opened his mouth and blew softly down into his lungs.

I repeated this a few times, then laid the pup on

his side in the basket. I was just thinking it was going to be no good when the little rib cage gave a sudden lift, then another and another.

"He's off!" Bert exclaimed happily. "That's champion! We want these puppies alive tha knows. They're Jack Dennison's terrier and he's a grand 'un."

"That's right," Mrs. Chapman put in. "No matter how many she has, they're all spoken for. Everybody wants a pup out of Susie."

"I can believe that," I said. But I smiled to myself. Jack Dennison's terrier was another hound of uncertain ancestry, so this lot would be a right mixture, but none the worse for that.

I gave Susie half a c.c. of pituitrin. "I think she needs it after pushing against that fellow for hours. We'll wait and see what happens now."

And it was nice waiting. Mrs. Chapman brewed a pot of tea and began to slap butter onto homemade scones. Susie, partly aided by my pituitrin, pushed out a pup in a self-satisfied manner about every fifteen minutes. The pups themselves soon set up a bawling of surprising volume for such minute creatures.

Bert, relaxing visibly with every minute, filled his pipe and regarded the fast-growing family with a grin of increasing width. "Ee, it is kind of you young folks to stay with us like this."

Mrs. Chapman put her head on one side and looked at us worriedly. "I should think you've been dying to get back to your dance all this time."

I thought of the crush at the Drovers'. The smoke, the heat, the nonstop boom-boom of the Hot Shots and I looked around the peaceful little room with old-fashioned black grate, the low, varnished beams, Mrs. Chapman's sewing box, the row of Bert's pipes on the wall. I took a firmer grasp of Helen's hand which I had been holding under the table for the last hour.

"Not at all, Mrs. Chapman," I said. "We haven't missed it in the least." And I have never been more sincere.

It must have been about half past two when I finally decided that Susie had finished. She had six fine pups which was a good score for a little thing like her and the noise had abated as the family settled down to feast on her abundant udder.

I lifted the pups out one by one and examined them. Susie didn't mind in the least but appeared to be smiling with modest pride as I handled her brood. When I put them back with her she inspected them and sniffed them over busily before rolling onto her side again.

"Three dogs and three bitches," I said. "Nice even litter."

Before leaving I took Susie from her basket and palpated her abdomen. The degree of deflation was almost unbelievable; a pricked balloon could not have altered its shape more spectacularly and she had made a remarkable metamorphosis to the lean, scruffy little extrovert I knew so well. When I released her she scurried back and curled herself round her new family who were soon sucking away with total absorption.

Bert laughed. "She's fair capped wi' them pups." He bent over and prodded the first arrival with a horny forefinger. "I like the look o' this big dog pup. I reckon we'll keep this 'un for ourselves, Mother. He'll be company for t'awd lass."

It was time to go. Helen and I moved over to the door and little Mrs. Chapman with her fingers on the handle looked up at me. "Well, Mr. Herriot," she said, "I can't thank you enough for comin' out and putting our minds at rest. I don't know what I'd've done wi' this man of mine if anything had happened to his little dog."

Bert grinned sheepishly. "Nay," he muttered. "Ah was never really worried."

His wife laughed and opened the door and as we stepped out into the silent scented night she gripped my arm and looked up at me roguishly.

"I suppose this is your young lady," she said.

I put my arm round Helen's shoulders.

"Yes," I said firmly, "this is my young lady."

A Real Happy Harry

The first time I saw Phin Calvert was in the street outside the surgery when I was talking to Brigadier Julian Coutts-Browne about his shooting dogs. The brigadier was almost a stage version of an English aristocrat; immensely tall with a pronounced stoop, hawk features and high, drawling voice. As he spoke, smoke from a narrow cigar trickled from his lips.

I turned my head at the clatter of heavy boots on the pavement. A thick-set figure was stumping rapidly toward us, hands tucked behind his braces, ragged jacket pulled wide to display a curving expanse of collarless shirt, wisps of grizzled hair hanging in a fringe beneath a greasy cap. He was smiling widely at nobody in particular and he hummed busily to himself.

The brigadier glanced at him. "Morning, Calvert," he grunted coldly.

Phineas threw up his head in pleased recognition. "Now then, Charlie, 'ow is ta?" he shouted.

The brigadier looked as though he had swallowed a swift pint of vinegar. He removed his cigar with a shaking hand and stared after the retreating back. "Impudent devil," he muttered.

Looking at Phin, you would never have thought he was a prosperous farmer. I was called to his place a week later and was surprised to find a substantial house and buildings and a fine dairy herd grazing in the fields.

I could hear him even before I got out of the car.

"Hello, 'ello, 'ello! Who's this we've got then? New chap eh? Now we're going to learn summat!" He still had his hands inside his braces and was grinning wider than ever.

"My name is Herriot," I said.

"Is it now?" Phin cocked his head and surveyed me, then he turned to three young men standing by. "Hasn't he a nice smile, lads? He's a real Happy Harry!"

He turned and began to lead the way across the yard. "Come on, then, and we'll see what you're made of. I 'ope you know a bit about calves because I've got some here that are right dowly."

As he went into the calf house I was hoping I would be able to do something impressive—perhaps use some of the new drugs I had in my car; it was going to take something special to make an impact here.

There were six well-grown young animals, almost stirk size, and three of them were behaving very strangely, grinding their teeth, frothing at the mouth and blundering about the pen as though they couldn't see. As I watched, one of them walked straight into the wall and stood with its nose pressed against the stone.

Phin, apparently unconcerned, was humming to himself in a corner. When I started to take my thermometer from its case he burst into a noisy commentary. "Now what's he doing? Ah, we're off now, get up there!"

The half-minute spent taking an animal's temperature is usually devoted to hectic thought. But his time I didn't need the time to work out my diagnosis; the blindness made it easy. I began to look round the walls of the calf house; it was dark and I had to get my face close to the stone.

Phin gave tongue again. "Hey, what's going on? You're as bad as t'calves, nosing about there, dozy like. What d'you think you're lookin' for?"

"Paint, Mr. Calvert. I'm very sure your calves have got lead poisoning."

Phin said what all farmers say at this juncture. "They can't have. I've had calves in here for thirty years and they've never taken any harm before. There's no paint in here, anyway."

"How about this, then?" I peered into the darkest corner and pulled at a piece of loose board.

"Oh, that's nobbut a bit of wood I nailed down there

last week to block up a hole. Came off an old henhouse."

I looked at the twenty-year-old paint hanging off in the loose flakes which calves find so irresistible. "This is what's done the damage," I said. "Look, you can see the tooth marks where they've been at it."

Phin studied the board at close quarters and grunted doubtfully. "All right, what do we do now?"

"First thing is to get this painted board out of here and then give all the calves Epsom salts. Have you got any?"

Phin gave a bark of laughter. "Aye, I've got a bloody great sack full, but can't you do owt better than that? Aren't you going to inject them?"

It was a little embarrassing. The specific antidotes to metal poisoning had not yet been discovered and the only thing which sometimes did a bit of good was magnesium sulfate. The homely term for magnesium sulfate is, of course, Epsom salts.

"No," I said. "There's nothing I can inject that will help at all and I can't even guarantee the salts will. But I'd like you to give the calves two heaped table-spoonfuls three times a day."

"Oh 'ell, you'll skitter the poor beggars to death!"

"Maybe so, but there's nothing else for it," I said.

Phin took a step toward me so that his face, dark-skinned and deeply wrinkled, was close to mine. The suddenly shrewd, mottled brown eyes regarded me steadily for a few seconds, then he turned away quickly. "Right," he said. "Come in and have a drink."

Phin stumped into the farm kitchen ahead of me, threw back his head and let loose a bellow that shook the windows. "Mother! Feller 'ere wants a glass o' beer. Come and meet Happy Harry!"

Mrs. Calvert appeared with magical speed and put down glasses and bottles. I glanced at the labels— "Smith's Nutty Brown Ale"—and filled my glass. It was a historic moment though I didn't know it then; it was the first of an incredible series of Nutty Browns I was to drink at that table.

Mrs. Calvert sat down for a moment, crossed her hands on her lap and smiled encouragingly. "Can you do anything for the calves, then?" she asked.

Phin butted in before I could reply. "Oh aye, he can an' all. He's put them onto Epsom salts."

"Epsom salts?"

"That's it, missis. I said when he came that we'd get summat real smart and scientific-like. You can't beat new blood and modern ideas." Phin sipped his beer gravely.

Over the following days the calves gradually improved and at the end of a fortnight they were all eating normally. The worst one still showed a trace of blindness, but I was confident this too would clear up.

It wasn't long before I saw Phin again. It was early afternoon and I was in the office with Siegfried when the outer door banged and the passage echoed to the clumping of hobnails. I heard a voice raised in song—hi-ti-tid-dly-rum-te-tum. Phineas was in our midst once more.

"Well, well, well!" he bawled heartily at Miss

Harbottle, our secretary. "It's Flossie! And what's my little darlin' doing this fine day?"

There was not a flicker from Miss Harbottle's granite features. She directed an icy stare at the intruder but Phin swung round on Siegfried with a yellow-toothed grin. "Now, gaffer, 'ow's tricks?"

"Everything's fine, Mr. Calvert," Siegfried replied. "What can we do for you?"

Phin stabbed a finger at me. "There's my man. I want him out to my place right sharpish."

"What's the trouble?" I asked. "Is it the calves again?"

"Damn, no! Wish it was. It's me good bull. He's puffin' like a bellows—bit like pneumonia but worse than I've known. He's in a 'ell of a state. Looks like he's peggin' out." For an instant Phin lost his jocularity.

I had heard of this bull; pedigree shorthorn, show winner, the foundation of his herd. "I'll be right after you, Mr. Calvert. I'll follow you along."

"Good lad. I'm off, then." Phin paused at the door, a wild figure, tieless, tattered; baggy trousers ballooning from his ample middle.

He turned again to Miss Harbottle and contorted his leathery features into a preposterous leer. "Ta-ra, Floss!" he cried and was gone.

For a moment the room seemed very empty and quiet except for Miss Harbottle's acid "Oh, that man! Dreadful! Dreadful!"

I made good time to the farm and found Phin waiting with his three sons. The young men looked gloomy but Phin was still indomitable. "Here 'e is!" he shouted. "Happy Harry again. Now we'll be all right." He even managed a little tune as we crossed to the bull pen but when he looked over the door his head sank on his chest and his hands worked deeper behind his braces.

The bull was standing as though rooted to the middle of the pen. His great rib cage rose and fell with the most labored respirations I had ever seen. His mouth gaped wide, a bubbling foam hung round his lips and his flaring nostrils; his eyes, almost starting from his head in terror, stared at the wall in front of him. This wasn't pneumonia, it was a frantic battle for breath; and it looked like a losing one.

He didn't move when I inserted my thermometer and though my mind was racing I suspected the half-minute wasn't going to be long enough this time. I had expected accelerated breathing, but nothing like this.

"Poor aud beggar," Phin muttered. "He's bred me the fittest calves I've ever had and he's as quiet as a sheep, too. I've seen me little grandchildren walk under 'is belly and he's took no notice. I hate to see him sufferin' like this. If you can't do no good, just tell me and I'll get the gun out."

I took out the thermometer and read it—110°F. This was ridiculous; I shook it vigorously and tried again.

I gave it nearly a minute this time so that I could get in some extra thinking. The second reading said 110°F again and I had an unpleasant conviction that if the thermometer had been a foot long the mercury would still have been jammed against the top.

What in the name of God was this? Could be anthrax . . . must be . . . and yet . . . I looked over at the row of heads above the half-door; they were waiting for me to say something and their silence accentuated the agonized groaning and panting. I looked above the heads to the square of deep blue and a tufted cloud moving across the sun. As it passed, a single dazzling ray made me close my eyes and a faint bell rang in my mind.

"Has he been out today?" I asked.

"Aye, he's been out on the grass on his tether all morning. It was that grand and warm."

The bell became a triumphant gong. "Get a hosepipe in here quick. You can rig it to the tap in the yard."

"A hosepipe? What the 'ell . . . ?"

"Yes, quick as you can—he got sunstroke."

They had the hose fixed in less than a minute. I

turned it full on and began to play the jet of cold water all over the huge form—his face and neck, along the ribs, up and down the legs. I kept this up for about five minutes but it seemed a lot longer as I waited for some sign of improvement. I was beginning to think I was on the wrong track when the bull gulped just once.

It was something—he had been unable to swallow his saliva before, in his desperate efforts to get air into his lungs; and I really began to notice a change in the big animal. Surely he was looking just a little less distressed and wasn't the breathing slowing down a bit?

Then the bull shook himself, turned his head and looked at us. There was an awed whisper from one of the young men: "By gaw, it's working!"

I enjoyed myself after that. I can't think of anything in my working life that has given me more pleasure than standing in that pen directing the life-saving jet and watching the bull savoring it. He liked it on his face best and as I worked my way up from the tail and along the steaming back he would turn his nose full into the water, rocking his head from side to side and blinking blissfully.

Within half an hour he looked almost normal. His chest was still heaving a little but he was in no discomfort. I tried the temperature again. Down to 105°F.

"He'll be all right now," I said. "But I think one of the lads should keep the water on him for another twenty minutes or so. I'll have to go now."

"You've time for a drink," Phin grunted.

In the farm kitchen his bellow of "Mother" lacked some of its usual timbre. He dropped into a chair and stared into his glass of Nutty Brown. "Harry," he said, "I'll tell you, you've flummoxed me this time." He sighed and rubbed his chin in apparent disbelief. "I don't know what the 'ell to say to you."

It wasn't often that Phin lost his voice, but he found it again very soon at the next meeting of the farmers' discussion group.

A learned and earnest gentleman had been expounding on the advances in veterinary medicine and how the farmers could now expect their stock to be treated as the doctors treated their human patients, with the newest drugs and procedures.

It was too much for Phin. He jumped to his feet and cried: "Ah think you're talking a lot of rubbish. There's a young feller in Darrowby not long out of college and it doesn't matter what you call 'im out for he uses nowt but Epsom salts and cold water."

Mick
the Dreamer

It was nine o'clock on a filthy wet night and I was still at work. I gripped the steering wheel more tightly and shifted in my seat, groaning softly as my tired muscles complained.

Why had I entered this profession? I could have gone in for something easier and gentler—like coalmining or lumberjacking. I had started feeling sorry for myself three hours ago, driving across Darrowby marketplace on the way to calving. The shops were shut and even through the wintry drizzle there was a suggestion of repose, of work done, of firesides and books and drifting tobacco smoke. I had all those things, plus Helen, back there in our bed-sitter at the top of Skeldale House.

I think the iron really entered when I saw the car-load of young people setting off from the front of the

Drovers' Arms; three girls and three young fellows, all dressed up and laughing and obviously on their way to a dance or party. Everybody was set for comfort and a good time; everybody except Herriot, rattling toward the cold wet hills and the certain prospect of toil.

And the case did nothing to raise my spirits. A skinny little heifer stretched on her side in a ramshackle open-fronted shed littered with old tin cans, half-bricks and other junk; it was difficult to see what I was stumbling over since the only light came from a rusty old lamp whose flame flickered and dipped in the wind.

I was two hours in that shed, easing out the calf inch by inch. It wasn't a malpresentation, just a tight fit, but the heifer never rose to her feet and I spent the whole time on the floor, rolling among the bricks and tins, getting up only to shiver my way to the water bucket while the rain hurled itself icily against the shrinking flesh of my chest and back.

And now here I was, driving home frozen-faced with my skin chafing under my clothes and feeling as though a group of strong men had been kicking me enthusiastically from head to foot for most of the evening. I was almost drowning in self-pity when I turned into the tiny village of Copton. In the warm days of summer it was idyllic, reminding me always of a corner of Perthshire, with its single street hugging the lower slopes of a green hillside and a dark drift of trees spreading to the heathery uplands high above.

But tonight it was a dead black place with the rain sweeping across the headlights against the tight-shut houses, except for a faint glow right in the middle where the light from the village pub fell softly on the streaming roadway. I stopped the car under the swinging sign of the Fox and Hounds and, on an impulse, opened the door. A beer would do me good.

A pleasant warmth met me as I went into the pub. There was no bar counter, only high-backed settles and oak tables arranged under the whitewashed walls of what was simply a converted farm kitchen. At one end a wood fire crackled in an old black cooking range and above it the tick of a wall clock sounded above the murmur of voices. It wasn't as lively as the modern places but it was peaceful.

"Now then, Mr. Herriot, you've been workin'," my neighbor said as I sank onto the settle.

"Yes, Ted, how did you know?"

The man glanced over my soiled overcoat and the boots I hadn't bothered to change on the farm. "Well, that's not your Sunday suit, there's blood on your nose end and cow muck on your ear." Ted Dobson was a burly cowman in his thirties and his white teeth showed suddenly in a wide grin.

I smiled too and plied my handkerchief. "It's funny how you always want to scratch your nose at times like that."

I looked around the room. There were about a dozen men drinking from pint glasses, some of them playing dominoes. They were all farm workers, the people I saw when I was called from my bed in the darkness before dawn; hunched figures they were then, shapeless in old greatcoats, cycling out to the farms, heads down against the wind and rain, accepting the facts of their hard existence. I often thought at those times that this happened to me only occasionally, but they did it every morning.

And they did it for thirty shillings a week; just seeing them here made me feel a little ashamed.

Mr. Waters, the landlord, whose name let him in for a certain amount of ribbing, filled my glass, holding his tall jug high to produce the professional froth.

"There y'are, Mr. Herriot, that'll be sixpence. Cheap at 'alf the price."

Every drop of beer was brought up in that jug from the wooden barrels in the cellar. It would have been totally impracticable in a busy establishment, but the Fox and Hounds was seldom bustling and Mr. Waters would never get rich as a publican. But he had four cows in the little byre adjoining this room, fifty hens pecked around in his long back garden and he reared a few litters of pigs every year from his two sows.

"Thank you, Mr. Waters." I took a deep pull at the glass. I had lost some sweat despite the cold and my thirst welcomed the flow of rich nutty ale. I had been in here a few times before and the faces were all familiar. Especially old Albert Close, a retired shepherd who sat in the same place every night at the end of the settle hard against the fire.

He sat as always, his hands and chin resting on the tall crook which he had carried through his working days, his eyes blank. Stretched half under the seat, half under the table lay his dog, Mick, old and retired like his master. The animal was clearly in the middle of a vivid dream; his paws pedaled the air spasmodically, his lips and ears twitched and now and then he emitted a stifled bark.

Ted Dobson nudged me and laughed. "Ah reckon awd Mick's still rounding up them sheep."

I nodded. There was little doubt the dog was reliving the great day, crouching and darting, speeding in a wide arc round the perimeter of the field at his master's whistle. And Albert himself. What lay behind those empty eyes? I could imagine him in his youth, striding the windy uplands, covering endless miles over moor and rock and beck, digging that same crook into the turf at every step. There were no fitter men than the Dales shepherds, living in the open in all weathers, throwing a sack over their shoulders in snow and rain.

And there was Albert now, a broken, arthritic old man gazing apathetically from beneath the ragged peak of an ancient tweed cap. I noticed he had just drained his glass and I walked across the room.

"Good evening, Mr. Close," I said.

He cupped an ear with his hand and blinked up at

me. "Eh?" I raised my voice to a shout. "How are you, Mr. Close?"

"Can't complain, young man," he murmured. "Can't complain."

"Will you have a drink?"

"Aye, thank ye." He directed a trembling finger at his glass. "You can put a drop i' there, young man."

I knew a drop meant a pint and beckoned to the landlord who plied his jug expertly. The old shepherd lifted the recharged glass and looked up at me. "Good 'ealth," he grunted.

"All the best," I said and was about to return to my seat when the old dog sat up. My shouts at his master must have wakened him from his dream because he stretched sleepily, shook his head a couple of times and looked around him. And as he turned and faced me I felt a sudden sense of shock.

His eyes were terrible. In fact I could hardly see them as they winked painfully at me through a sodden fringe of dirt-caked lashes. Rivulets of discharge showed dark and ugly against the white hair on either side of the nose.

I stretched my hand out to him and the dog wagged his tail briefly before closing his eyes and keeping them closed. It seemed he felt better that way.

I put my hand on Albert's shoulder. "Mr. Close, how long has he been like this?"

"Eh?"

I increased my volume. "Mick's eyes. They're in a bad state."

"Oh, aye." The old man nodded in comprehension. "He's got a bit o' caud in 'em. He allus been subjeck to it ever since 'e were a pup."

"No, it's more than cold, it's his eyelids."

"Eh?"

I took a deep breath and let go at the top of my voice. "He's got turned-in eyelids. It's rather a serious thing."

The old man nodded again. "Aye, 'e lies a lot wi' his head at foot of t'door. It's draughty there."

"No, Mr. Close!" I bawled. "It's got nothing to do with that. It's a thing called entropion and it needs an operation to put it right."

"That's right, young man." He took a sip at his beer. "Just a bit o' caud. Ever since he were a pup he's been subjeck . . ."

I turned away wearily and returned to my seat. Ted Dobson looked at me inquiringly. "What was that about?"

"Well, it's a nasty thing, Ted. Entropion is when the eyelids are turned in and the lashes rub against the eyeball. Causes a lot of pain, sometimes ulceration or even blindness. Even a mild case is damned uncomfortable for a dog."

"I see," Ted said ruminatively. "Ah've noticed awd Mick's had mucky eyes for a long time but they've got worse lately."

"Yes, sometimes it happens like that, but often it's congenital. I should think Mick has had a touch of it all his life but for some reason it's suddenly developed to this horrible state." I turned again toward the old dog, sitting patiently under the table, eyes still tight shut.

"He's sufferin' then!"

I shrugged my shoulders. "Well, you know what it's like if you have a speck of dust in your eyes or even one lash turned in. I should say he feels pretty miserable."

"Poor awd beggar. Ah never knew it was owt like that." He drew on his cigarette. "And could an operation cure it?"

"Yes, Ted, it's one of the most satisfying jobs a vet can do. I always feel I've done a dog a good turn when I've finished."

"Aye, ah bet you do. It must be a nice feelin'. But it'll be a costly job, ah reckon?"

I smiled wryly. "It depends how you look at it. It's a fiddly business and takes time. We usually charge about a pound for it." A human surgeon would laugh at a sum like that, but it would still be too much for old Albert.

For a few moments we were both silent, looking across the room at the old man, at the threadbare coat, the long tatter of trouser bottoms falling over the broken boots. A pound would amount to two weeks of his old-age pension. It was a fortune.

Ted got up suddenly. "Any road, somebody ought to tell 'im. Ah'll explain it to 'im."

He crossed the room. "Are ye ready for another, Albert?"

The old shepherd glanced at him absently, then indicated his glass, empty again. "Aye, ye can put a drop i' there, Ted."

The cowman waved to Mr. Waters, then bent down. "Did ye understand what Mr. Herriot was tellin' ye, Albert?" he shouted.

"Aye . . . aye . . . Mick's got a bit o' caud in 'is eyes."

"Nay, 'e hasn't! It's nowt a t'soart! It's a en . . . a en . . . summat different."

"Keeps gettin' caud in 'em," Albert mumbled, nose in glass.

Ted yelled in exasperation. "Ye daft awd divil! Listen to what ah'm sayin—ye've got to take care of 'im and . . ."

But the old man was far away. "Ever sin 'e were a pup . . . allus been subjeck to it. . . ."

Although Mick took my mind off my own troubles at the time, the memory of those eyes haunted me for days. I yearned to get my hands on them. I knew an hour's work would transport the old dog into a world he perhaps had not known for years, and every instinct told me to rush back to Copton, throw him in the car and bear him back to Darrowby for surgery. I wasn't worried about the money but you just can't run a practice that way.

I regularly saw lame dogs on farms, skinny cats on the streets and it would have been lovely to descend on each and every one and minister to them out of my knowledge. In fact I had tried a bit of it and it didn't work.

It was Ted Dobson who put me out of my pain. He had come into the town to see his sister for the evening and he stood leaning on his bicycle in the surgery doorway, his cheerful, scrubbed face gleaming as if it would light up the street.

He came straight to the point. "Will ye do that operation on awd Mick, Mr. Herriot?"

"Yes, of course, but . . . how about . . . ?"

"Oh that'll be right. T'lads at Fox and Hounds are seein' to it. We're takin' it out of the club money."

"Club money?"

"Aye, we put in a bit every week for an outin' in t'summer. Trip to t'seaside or summat like."

"Well it's extremely kind of you, Ted, but are you quite sure? Won't any of them mind?"

Ted laughed. "Nay, it's nowt, we won't miss a quid. We drink ower much on them do's anyway." He paused. "All t'lads want this job done—it's been gettin' on our bloody nerves ever since you told us about 'im."

"Well, that's great," I said. "How will you get him down?"

"Me boss is lendin' me 'is van. Wednesday night be all right?"

"Fine." I watched him ride away then turned back along the passage. It may seem to modern eyes that a lot of fuss had been made over a pound but in those days it was a very substantial sum, and some idea may be gained from the fact that four pounds a week was my commencing salary as a veterinary surgeon.

When Wednesday night arrived it was clear that Mick's operation had become something of a gala occasion. The little van was crammed with regulars from the Fox and Hounds and other rolled up on their bicycles.

The old dog slunk fearfully down the passage to the operation room, nostrils twitching at the unfamiliar odors of ether and antiseptic. Behind him trooped the noisy throng of farm men, their heavy boots clattering on the tiles.

Tristan, who was doing the anesthesia, hoisted the dog on the table and I looked around at the unusual spectacle of rows of faces regarding me with keen anticipation. Normally I am not in favor of lay people witnessing operations but since these men were sponsoring the whole thing they would have to stay.

Under the lamp I got my first good look at Mick. He was a handsome, well-marked animal except for those dreadful eyes. As he sat there he opened them a fraction and peered at me for a painful moment before closing them against the bright light; that, I felt, was how he spent his life, squinting carefully and briefly at his surroundings.

And when he was stretched unconscious on his side I was able to carry out my first examination. I parted the lids, wincing at the matted lashes, awash with tears and discharge; there was a longstanding keratitis and conjunctivitis but with a gush of relief I found that the cornea was not ulcerated.

"You know," I said, "this is a mess, but I don't think there's any permanent damage."

The farm men didn't exactly break into a cheer but they were enormously pleased. The carnival air was heightened as they chattered and laughed and when I poised my scalpel it struck me that I had never operated in such a noisy environment.

But I felt almost gleeful as I made the first incision; I had been looking forward so much to this moment. Starting with the left eye I cut along the full length parallel to the margin of the lid, then made a semi-circular sweep of the knife to include half an inch of the tissue above the eye. Seizing the skin with forceps I stripped it away, and as I drew the lips of the bleeding wound together with stitches I noticed with intense gratification how the lashes were pulled high and away from the corneal surface they had irritated, perhaps for years.

I cut away less skin from the lower lid—you never need to take so much there—then started on the right eye. I was slicing away happily when I realized that the noise had subsided; there were a few mutterings, but the chaff and laughter had died. Once the cutting was over, however, life slowly returned to the party.

"What a lot of pale faces. I think you could all do with a drop of whiskey," Tristan said after I had inserted the last stitch and we had begun to put away the instruments. He left the room and returned with a bottle which, with typical hospitality, he dispensed to all. Beakers, measuring glasses and test tubes were pressed into service and soon there was a boisterous throng around the sleeping dog. When the van finally roared off into the night the last thing I heard was the sound of singing from the packed interior.

They brought Mick back in ten days for removal of the stitches. The wounds had healed well but the keratitis had still not cleared and the old dog was still blinking painfully. I didn't see the final result of my work for another month.

It was when I was again driving home through Copton from an evening call that the lighted doorway of the Fox and Hounds recalled me to the little operation which had been almost forgotten in the rush of new work. I went in and sat down among the familiar faces.

Things were uncannily like before. Old Albert Close in his usual place, Mick stretched under the table, his twitching feet testifying to another vivid dream. I watched him closely until I could stand it no longer. As if drawn by a magnet I crossed the room and crouched by him.

"Mick!" I said. "Hey, wake up, boy!"

The quivering limbs stilled and there was a long moment when I held my breath as the shaggy head turned toward me. Then with a kind of blissful disbelief I found myself gazing into the wide, clear, bright eyes of a young dog.

Warm wine flowed richly through my veins as he faced me, mouth open in a panting grin, tail swishing along the stone flags. There was no inflammation, no discharge, and the lashes, clean and dry, grew in a soft arc well clear of the corneal surface which they had chafed and rasped for so long. I stroked his head and as he began to look around him eagerly I felt a thrill of utter delight, at the sight of the old animal exulting in his freedom, savoring the new world which had opened to him. I could see Ted Dobson and the other men smiling conspiratorially as I stood up.

"Mr. Close," I shouted, "will you have a drink?"

"Aye, you can put a drop i' there, young man."

"Mick's eyes are a lot better."

The old man raised his glass. "Good 'ealth. Aye, it were nobbut a bit o' caud."

"But Mr. Close . . . !"

"Nasty thing, is caud in t'eyes. T'awd feller keeps lyin' in that door'ole and ah reckon he'll get it again. Ever since 'e were a pup 'e's been subjeck . . ."

Blossom Comes Home

⁓

After the rigors of lambing during March and April, my world became softer and warmer through May and early June. At Skeldale House the wisteria exploded into a riot of mauve blooms which thrust themselves through the open windows and each morning as I shaved I breathed in the heady fragrance from the long clusters drooping by the side of the mirror. Life was idyllic.

At times it seemed unfair that I should be paid for my work; for driving out in the early morning with the fields glistening under the first pale sunshine and the wisps of mist still hanging on the high tops. The air, fresh as the sea, carried a faint breath of the thousands of wildflowers which speckled the pastures.

It was on such a morning that I arrived at Mr. Dakin's farm just outside Darrowby. I saw Mr. Dakin in the cow byre and went across to him. The farmer's patient eyes in the long, drooping mustached face looked down at me from his stooping height.

"It looks as though it's over wi' awd Blossom, then," he said, and rested his hand briefly on the old cow's back. It was an enormous, work-swollen hand. Mr. Dakin's gaunt frame carried little flesh but the grossly thickened fingers bore testimony to a life of toil.

I dried off the needle and dropped it into the metal box where I carried my suture materials, scalpels and blades. "Well, it's up to you of course, Mr. Dakin, but this is the third time I've had to stitch her teats and I'm afraid it's going to keep on happening."

"Aye, it's just the shape she is." The farmer bent and examined the row of knots along the four-inch scar. "By gaw, you wouldn't believe it could mek such a mess—just another cow standin' on it."

"A cow's hoof is sharp," I said. "It's nearly like a knife coming down."

That was the worst of very old cows. Their udders dropped and their teats became larger and more pendulous so that when they lay down in their stalls the vital milk-producing organ was pushed away to one side into the path of the neighboring animals. If it wasn't Mabel on the right standing on it, it was Buttercup on the other side.

There were only six cows in the little cobbled byre

with its low roof and wooden partitions and they all had names. You don't find cows with names anymore and there aren't any farmers like Mr. Dakin who somehow scratched a living from a herd of six milkers plus a few calves, pigs and hens.

"Aye, well," he said, "ah reckon t'awd lass doesn't owe me anythin'. Ah remember the night she was born, twelve years ago. She was out of awd Daisy and ah carried her out of this very byre on a sack and the snow was comin' down hard. Since then ah wouldn't like to count how many thousand gallons o' milk she's turned out—she's still givin' four a day. Naw, she doesn't owe me a thing."

As if she knew she was the topic of conversation Blossom turned her head and looked at him. She was the classical picture of an ancient bovine; as fleshless as her owner, with jutting pelvic bones, splayed, overgrown feet, and horns with a multitude of rings along their curving length. Beneath her, the udder, once high and tight, drooped forlornly almost to the floor.

She resembled her owner, too, in her quiet, patient demeanor. I had infiltrated her teat with a local anesthetic before stitching but I don't think she would have moved if I hadn't used any. Stitching teats puts a vet in the ideal position to be kicked, with his head low down in front of the hind feet, but there was no danger with Blossom. She had never kicked anybody in her life.

Mr. Dakin blew out his cheeks. "Well, there's nowt else for it. She'll have to go. I'll tell Jack Dodson to pick 'er up for the fatstock market on Thursday. She'll be a bit tough for eatin' but ah reckon she'll make a few steak pies."

He was trying to joke but he was unable to smile as he looked at the old cow. Behind him, beyond the open door, the green hillside ran down to the river and the spring sunshine touched the broad sweep of the shallows with a million dancing lights. A beach of bleached stones gleamed bone-white against the long stretch of grassy bank which rolled up to the pastures lining the valley floor. I had often felt that this small holding would be an ideal place to live; only a mile outside Darrowby, but secluded and with this heart-lifting vista of river and fell. I remarked on this once to Mr. Dakin and the old man turned to me with a wry smile. "Aye, but the view's not very sustainin'," he said.

It happened that I was called back to the farm on the following Thursday to check over a cow and was in the byre when Dodson the drover called to pick up Blossom. He had collected a group of fat bullocks and cows from other farms and they stood, watched by one of his men, on the road high above.

"Nah then, Mr. Dakin," he cried as he bustled in, "it's easy to see which one you want me to tek. It's that awd screw over there."

He pointed at Blossom, and in truth the unkind description seemed to fit the bony creature standing between her sleek neighbors.

The farmer did not reply for a moment, then he went up between the cows and gently rubbed Blossom's forehead. "Aye, this is the one, Jack." He hesitated, then undid the chain round her neck. "Off ye go, awd lass," he murmured, and the old animal turned and made her way placidly from the stall.

"Aye, come on with ye!" shouted the dealer, poking his stick against the cow's rump.

"Don't hit 'er!" barked Mr. Dakin.

Dodson looked at him in surprise. "Ah never 'it 'em, you know that. Just send 'em on, like."

"Ah knaw, ah knaw, Jack, but you won't need your stick for this 'un. She'll go wherever ye want—allus has done."

Blossom confirmed his words as she ambled through the door and, at a gesture from the farmer, turned along the track.

The old man and I stood watching as the cow made her way unhurriedly up the hill, Jack Dodson in his long khaki smock sauntering behind her. As the path wound behind a clump of sparse trees man and beast disappeared but Mr. Dakin still gazed after them, listening to the clip-clop of the hooves on the hard ground.

When the sound died away he turned to me quickly. "Right, Mr. Herriot, let's get on wi' our job, then."

The farmer was silent as I inspected the cow inside and out. He responded to my sallies on the weather, cricket and the price of milk with a series of grunts. Holding the cow's tail he leaned on the hairy back and, empty-eyed, blew smoke from his pipe.

At last I was finished. I untied the sack from my middle and pulled my shirt over my head. All conversation died and the silence was almost oppressive as we opened the byre door.

Mr. Dakin paused, his hand on the latch. "What's that?" he said softly.

From somewhere on the hillside I could hear the

clip-clop of a cow's feet. There were two ways to the farm and the sound came from a narrow track which joined the main road half a mile beyond the other entrance. As we listened a cow rounded a rocky outcrop and came toward us.

It was Blossom, moving at a brisk trot, great udder swinging, eyes fixed purposefully on the open door behind us.

"What the hangment . . . ?" Mr. Dakin burst out, but the old cow brushed past us and marched without hesitation into the stall which she had occupied for all those years. She sniffed inquiringly at the empty hay rack and looked round at her owner.

Mr. Dakin stared back at her. The eyes in the weathered face were expressionless but the smoke rose from his pipe in a series of rapid puffs.

Heavy boots clattered suddenly outside and Jack Dodson panted his way through the door.

"Oh, you're there, ye awd beggar!" he gasped. "Ah thought I'd lost ye!"

He turned to the farmer. "By gaw, I'm sorry, Mr. Dakin. She must 'ave turned off at t'top of your other path. Ah never saw her go."

The farmer shrugged. "It's awright, Jack. It's not your fault, ah should've told ye."

"That's soon mended anyway." The drover grinned and moved toward Blossom. "Come on, lass, let's have ye out o' there again."

But he halted as Mr. Dakin held an arm in front of him.

There was a long silence as Dodson and I looked in surprise at the farmer who continued to gaze fixedly at the cow. There was a pathetic dignity about the old animal as she stood there against the moldering timber of the partition, her eyes patient and demanding. It was a dignity which triumphed over the unsightliness of the long upturned hooves, the fleshless ribs, the broken-down udder almost brushing the cobbles.

Then, still without speaking, Mr. Dakin moved unhurriedly between the cows and a faint chink of metal sounded as he fastened the chain around Blossom's neck. Then he strolled to the end of the byre and returned with a forkful of hay which he tossed expertly into the rack.

This was what Blossom was waiting for. She jerked a mouthful from between the spars and began to chew with quiet satisfaction.

"What's to do, Mr. Dakin?" the drover cried in bewilderment. "They're waiting for me at t'mart!"

The farmer tapped out his pipe on the half-door

and began to fill it with black shag from a battered tin. "Ah'm sorry to waste your time, Jack, but you'll have to go without 'er."

"Without 'er . . . ? But . . . ?"

"Aye, ye'll think I'm daft, but that's how it is. T'awd lass has come 'ome and she's stoppin' 'ome." He directed a look of flat finality at the drover.

Dodson nodded a couple of times then shuffled from the byre. Mr. Dakin followed and called after him. "Ah'll pay ye for your time, Jack. Put it down on ma bill."

He returned, applied a match to his pipe and drew deeply.

"Mr. Herriot," he said as the smoke rose around his ears, "do you ever feel when summat happens that it was meant to happen and that it was for t'best?"

"Yes, I do, Mr. Dakin. I often feel that."

"Aye well, that's how I felt when Blossom came down that hill." He reached out and scratched the root of the cow's tail. "She's allus been a favorite and by gaw I'm glad she's back."

"But how about those teats? I'm willing to keep stitching them up, but. . . ."

"Nay, lad, ah've had an idea. Just came to me, but I thowt I was ower late."

"An idea?"

"Aye." The old man nodded and tamped down the tobacco with his thumb. "I can put two or three calves on to 'er instead of milkin' 'er. The old stable is empty—she can live in there where there's nobody to stand on 'er awd tits."

I laughed. "You're right, Mr. Dakin. She'd be safe in the stable and she'd suckle three calves easily. She could pay her way."

"Well, as ah said, it's matterless. After all them years she doesn't owe me a thing." A gentle smile spread over the seamed face. "Main thing is, she's come 'ome."

There's Nothing Wrong with Myrtle

~~~~

"Oooh . . . ooh-hoo-hooo!" The broken-hearted sobbing jerked me into full wakefulness. It was 1:00 A.M. and after the familiar jangling of the bedside phone I expected the gruff voice of a farmer with a calving cow. Instead, there was this terrible sound.

"Who is this?" I asked, a little breathlessly. "What on earth is the trouble?"

I heard a gulping at the other end and then a man's voice pleading between sobs. "It's Humphrey Cobb. For God's sake come out and see Myrtle. I think she's dyin'."

"Myrtle?"

"Aye, me poor little dog. She's in a 'ell of a state! Oooh-hooo!"

The receiver trembled in my grasp. "What is she doing?"

"Oh, pantin' and gaspin'. I think it's nearly all over with 'er. Come quick!"

"Where do you live?"

"Cedar House. End of Hill Street."

"I know it. I'll be there very soon."

"Oh, thank ye, thank ye. Myrtle hasn't got long. Hurry, hurry!"

I leaped from the bed and rushed at my clothes, draped over a chair against the wall. In my haste, in the darkness, I got both feet down one leg of my working corduroys and crashed full length on the floor.

Helen was used to nocturnal calls and often she only half woke. For my part I always tried to avoid disturbing her by dressing without switching on the light; there was always a glow from the nightlight we kept burning on the landing for young Jimmy.

However, the system broke down this time. The thud of my falling body brought her into a sitting position.

"What is it, Jim? What's happening?"

I struggled to my feet. "It's all right, Helen, I just tripped over." I snatched my shirt from the chair back.

"But what are you dashing about for?"

"Desperately urgent case. I have to hurry."

"All right, Jim, but you won't get there any sooner by going on like this. Just calm down."

My wife was right, of course. I have always envied

those vets who can stay relaxed under pressure. But I wasn't made that way.

I galloped down the stairs and through the long back garden to the garage. Cedar House was only a mile away and I didn't have much time to think about the case, but by the time I arrived I had pretty well decided that acute breathlessness like this would probably be caused by a heart attack or some sudden allergy.

In answer to my ring the porch light flashed on and Humphrey Cobb stood before me. He was a little round man in his sixties and his humpty-dumpty appearance was accentuated by his gleaming bald head.

"Oh, Mr. Herriot, come in, come in," he cried brokenly as the tears streamed down his cheeks. "Thank ye for gettin' out of your bed to help me poor little Myrtle."

As he spoke, the blast of whiskey fumes almost made my head spin and I noticed that as he preceded me across the hall he staggered slightly.

My patient was lying in a basket by the side of an Aga stove in a large, well-appointed kitchen. I felt a warm surge when I saw that she was a beagle like my own dog, Sam. I knelt down and looked at her closely. Her mouth was open and her tongue lolled, but she did not seem to be in acute distress. In fact, as I patted her head her tail flapped against the blanket.

A heart-rending wail sounded in my ear. "What d'ye make of her, Mr. Herriot? It's her heart, isn't it? Oh, Myrtle, Myrtle!"

The little man crouched over his pet and the tears flowed unchecked.

"You know, Mr. Cobb," I said, "she doesn't seem all that bad to me, so don't upset yourself too much. Just give me a chance to examine her."

I placed my stethoscope over the ribs and listened to the steady thudding of a superbly strong heart. The temperature was normal and I was palpating the abdomen when Mr. Cobb broke in again.

"The trouble is," he gasped, "I neglect this poor little animal."

"What do you mean?"

"Well, ah've been all day at Catterick at the races, gamblin' and drinkin' with never a thought for me dog."

"You left her alone all that time in the house?"

"Nay, nay, t'missus has been with her."

"Well, then"—I felt I was getting out of my depth—"she would feed Myrtle and let her out in the garden?" "Oh aye," he said, wringing his hands, "but I shouldn't leave 'er. She thinks such a lot about me."

As he spoke, I could feel one side of my face tingling with heat. My problem was suddenly solved.

"You've got her too near the Aga," I said. "She's panting because she's uncomfortably hot."

He looked at me doubtfully. "We just shifted 'er basket today. We've been gettin' some new tiles put down on the floor."

"Right," I said. "Shift it back again and she'll be fine."

"But, Mr. Herriot," his lips began to tremble again, "it's more than that. She's sufferin'. Look at her eyes."

Myrtle had the lovely big liquid eyes of her breed and she knew how to use them. Many people think the spaniel is number one when it comes to looking soulful but I personally plump for the beagle. And Myrtle was an expert.

"Oh, I wouldn't worry about that, Mr. Cobb," I said. "Believe me, she'll be all right."

He still seemed unhappy. "But aren't ye going to do something?"

It was one of the great questions in veterinary practice. If you didn't "do something" they were not satisfied. And in this case Mr. Cobb was in greater need of treatment than his pet. Still, I wasn't going to stick a needle into Myrtle just to please him, so I produced a vitamin tablet from my bag and pushed it over the back of the little animal's tongue.

"There you are," I said. "I'm sure that will do her good." And after all, I thought, I wasn't a complete charlatan—it wouldn't do her any harm.

Mr. Cobb relaxed visibly. "Eee, that's champion. You've set me mind at rest." He led the way into a luxurious drawing room and tacked unsteadily toward a cocktail cabinet. "You'll 'ave a drink before you go?"

"No, really, thanks," I said. "I'd rather not, if you don't mind."

"Well, I'll 'ave a drop. Just to steady me nerves. I was that upset." He tipped a lavish measure of whiskey into a glass and waved me to a chair.

My bed was calling me, but I sat down and watched as he drank. He told me that he was a retired bookmaker from the West Riding and that he had come to Darrowby only a month ago. Although no longer directly connected with horse racing he still loved the sport and never missed a meeting in the north of England.

"I allus get a taxi to take me and I have a right good day." His face was radiant as he recalled the happy times, then for a moment his cheeks quivered and his woebegone expression returned.

"But I neglect me dog. I leave her at home."

"Oh nonsense," I said. "I've seen you out in the fields with Myrtle. You give her plenty of exercise, don't you?"

"Oh aye, lots of walks every day."

"Well, then, she really has a good life. This is just a silly little notion you've got."

He beamed at me and sloshed out another few fingers of whiskey.

"Eee, you're a good lad. Come on, you'll just have one before you go."

"Oh, all right, just a small one, then."

As we drank he became more and more benign until he was gazing at me with something like devotion.

"James Herriot," he slurred. "I suppose it'll be Jim, eh?"

"Well, yes."

"I'll call you Jim, then, and you can call me Humphrey."

"Okay, Humphrey," I said, and swallowed the last of my whiskey. "But I really must go now."

Out in the street again he put a hand on my arm and his face became serious again. "Thank ye, Jim. Myrtle was right bad tonight and I'm grateful."

Driving away, I realized that I had failed to convince him that there was nothing wrong with his dog. He was sure I had saved her life. It had been an unusual visit and as my 2:00 A.M. whiskey burned in my stomach I decided that Humphrey Cobb was a very funny little man. But I liked him.

＊　　　＊　　　＊

After that night I saw him quite frequently exercising Myrtle in the fields. With his almost spherical build he seemed to bounce over the grass, but his manner was always self-contained and rational except that he kept thanking me for pulling his dog back from the jaws of death.

Then quite suddenly I was back at the beginning again. It was shortly after midnight and as I lifted the bedside phone I could hear the distraught weeping before the receiver touched my ear.

"Oooh . . . oooh . . . Jim, Jim. Myrtle's in a terrible bad way. Will ye come?"

"What . . . what is it this time?"

"She's twitchin'."

"Twitching?"

"Aye, twitchin' summat terrible. Oh, come on, Jim, lad, don't keep me waiting. I'm worried to death. I'm sure she's got distemper." He broke down again.

My head began to reel. "She can't have distemper, Humphrey. Not in a flash, like that."

"I'm beggin' you Jim," he went on as though he hadn't heard. "Be a pal. Come and see Myrtle."

"All right," I said wearily. "I'll be there in a few minutes."

"Oh, you're a good lad, Jim, you're a good lad. . . ." The voice trailed away as I replaced the phone. I dressed at normal speed with none of the panic of the first time. It sounded like a repetition, but why after midnight again? On my way to Cedar House I decided it must be another false alarm—but you never knew.

The same dizzying wave of whiskey fumes enveloped me in the porch. Humphrey, sniffling and moaning, fell against me once or twice as he ushered me into the kitchen. He pointed to the basket in the corner.

"There she is," he said, wiping his eyes. "I've just got back from Ripon and found 'er like this."

"Racing again, eh?"

"Aye, gamblin' on them 'osses and drinkin' and leavin' me poor dog pining at home. I'm a rotter, Jim, that's what I am."

"Rubbish, Humphrey! I've told you before. You're not doing her any harm by having a day out. Anyway, how about this twitching? She looks all right now."

"Yes, she's stopped doing it, but when I came in her back leg was goin' like this." He made a jerking movement with his hand.

I groaned inwardly. "But she could have been scratching or flicking away a fly."

"Nay, there's summat more than that. I can tell she's sufferin'. Just look at them eyes."

I could see what he meant. Myrtle's beagle eyes were pools of emotion and it was easy to read a melting reproach in their depths.

With a feeling of futility I examined her. I knew

what I would find—nothing. But when I tried to explain to the little man that his pet was normal he wouldn't have it.

"Oh, you'll give her one of them wonderful tablets," he pleaded. "It cured her last time."

I felt I had to pacify him, so Myrtle received another installment of vitamins.

Humphrey was immensely relieved and weaved his way to the drawing room and the whiskey bottle.

"I need a little pick-me-up after that shock," he said. "You'll 'ave one too, won't you, Jim lad?"

This pantomime was enacted frequently over the next few months, always after race meetings and always between midnight and 1:00 A.M. I had ample opportunity to analyze the situation and I came to a fairly obvious conclusion.

Most of the time Humphrey was a normal conscientious pet owner, but after a large intake of alcohol his affectionate feelings degenerated into a glutinous sentimentality and guilt. I invariably went out when he called me because I knew that he would be deeply distressed if I refused. I was treating Humphrey, not Myrtle.

It amused me that not once did he accept my protestations that my visit was unnecessary. Each time he was sure that my magic tablets had saved his dog's life.

Mind you, I did not discount the possibility that

Myrtle was deliberately working on him with those eyes. The canine mind is quite capable of disapproval. I took my own dog almost everywhere with me but if I left him at home to take Helen to the cinema he would lie under our bed, sulking, and when he emerged, would studiously ignore us for an hour or two.

I quailed when Humphrey told me he had decided to have Myrtle mated because I knew that the ensuing pregnancy would be laden with harassment for me. That was how it turned out. The little man flew into a series of alcoholic panics, all of them unfounded, and he discovered imaginary symptoms in Myrtle at regular intervals throughout the nine weeks.

I was vastly relieved when she gave birth to five healthy pups. Now, I thought, I would get some peace. The fact was that I was just about tired of Humphrey's

nocturnal nonsense. I have always made a point of never refusing to turn out at night but Humphrey had stretched this principle to breaking point. One of these times he would have to be told.

The crunch came when the pups were a few weeks old. I had had a terrible day, starting with a complicated calving at 5:00 A.M. and progressing through hours of road-slogging, missed meals and a late-night wrestle with government forms, some of which I suspected I had filled out wrongly.

My clerical incompetence has always infuriated me and when I crawled, dog tired, into bed my mind was still buzzing with frustration. I lay for a long time trying to put those forms away from me, and it was well after midnight when I fell asleep.

I have always had a silly fancy that our practice knows when I desperately want a full night's sleep. It knows and gleefully steps in. When the phone exploded in my ear I wasn't really surprised.

As I stretched a weary hand to the receiver the luminous dial of the alarm clock read 1:15 A.M.

"Hello," I grunted.

"Oooh . . . oooh . . . oooh!" The reply was only too familiar.

I clenched my teeth. This was just what I needed. "Humphrey! What is it this time?"

"Oh Jim, Myrtle's really dyin', I know she is. Come quick, lad, come quick!"

"Dying?" I took a couple of rasping breaths. "How do you make that out?"

"Well . . . she's stretched out on 'er side, tremblin'."

"Anything else?"

"Aye, t'missus said Myrtle's been looking worried and walkin' stiff when she let her out in the garden this afternoon. I'm not long back from Redcar, ye see?"

"So you've been to the races, eh?"

"That's right . . . neglectin' me dog. I'm a scamp, nothing but a scamp."

I closed my eyes in the darkness. There was no end to Humphrey's imaginary symptoms. Trembling, this time, looking worried, walking stiff. We'd had panting and twitching and head-nodding and ear-shaking—what would it be next?

But enough was enough. "Look, Humphrey," I said, "there's nothing wrong with your dog. I've told you again and again . . ."

"Oh, Jim, lad, don't be long. Ooooh-hooo!"

"I'm not coming, Humphrey."

"Nay, nay, don't say that! She's goin' fast, I tell ye!"

"I really mean it. It's just wasting my time and your money, so go to bed. Myrtle will be fine."

As I lay quivering between the sheets I realized that

refusing to go out was an exhausting business. There was no doubt in my mind that it would have taken less out of me to get up and attend another charade at Cedar House than to say "no" for the first time in my life. But this couldn't go on. I had to make a stand.

I was still tormented by remorse when I fell into an uneasy slumber and it is a good thing that the subconscious mind works on during sleep, because with the alarm clock reading 2:30 A.M. I came suddenly wide awake.

"My God!" I cried, staring at the dark ceiling. "Myrtle's got eclampsia!"

I scrambled from the bed and began to throw on my clothes. I must have made some commotion because I heard Helen's sleepy voice.

"What is it? What's the matter?"

"Humphrey Cobb!" I gasped, tying a shoe lace.

"Humphrey . . . but you said there was never any hurry . . ."

"There is this time. His dog's dying." I glared again at the clock. "In fact she could be dead now." I lifted my tie, then hurled it back on the chair. "Damn it! I don't need that." I fled from the room.

Down the long garden and into the car with my brain spelling out the concise case history which Humphrey had given me. Small bitch nursing five puppies, signs of anxiety and stiff gait this afternoon and now prostrate and trembling. Classical puerperal eclampsia. Rapidly fatal without treatment. And it was nearly an hour and a half since he had phoned. I couldn't bear to think about it.

Humphrey was still up. He had obviously been consoling himself with the bottle because he could barely stand.

"You've come, Jim lad," he mumbled, blinking at me.

"Yes, how is she?"

"Just t'same . . ."

Clutching my calcium and my intravenous syringe I rushed past him into the kitchen.

Myrtle's sleek body was extended in a tetanic spasm. She was gasping for breath, quivering violently, and bubbles of saliva dripped from her mouth. Those eyes had lost their softness and were fixed in a frantic stare. She looked terrible, but she was alive . . . she was alive.

I lifted the squealing pups onto a rug nearby and quickly clipped and swabbed the area over the radial vein. I inserted the needle into the blood vessel and began to depress the plunger with infinite care and very slowly. Calcium was the cure for this condition but a quick blast would surely kill the patient.

I took several minutes to empty the syringe then sat back on my heels and watched. Some of these cases needed drugs as well as calcium and I had Nembutal and morphine ready at hand. But as the time passed

Myrtle's breathing slowed down and the rigid muscles began to relax. When she started to swallow her saliva and look round at me I knew she would live.

I was waiting for the last tremors to disappear from her limbs when I felt a tap on my shoulder. Humphrey was standing there with the whiskey bottle in his hand.

"You'll 'ave one, won't you, Jim?"

I didn't need much persuading. The knowledge that I had almost been responsible for Myrtle's death had thrown me into a mild degree of shock.

My hand was still shaking as I raised the glass and I had barely taken the first sip when the little animal got up from the basket and walked over to inspect her pups. Some patients were slow to respond but others were spectacularly quick and I was grateful for the sake of my nervous system that this was one of the quick ones.

In fact the recovery was almost uncanny because, after sniffing her family over, Myrtle walked across the table to greet me. Her eyes brimmed with friendliness and her tail waved high in the true beagle fashion.

I was stroking her ears when Humphrey broke into a throaty giggle.

"You know, Jim, I've learned summat tonight." His voice was a slow drawl but he was still in possession of his wits.

"What's that, Humphrey?"

"I've learned . . . hee-hee-hee . . . I've learned what a silly feller I've been all these months."

"How do you mean?"

He raised a forefinger and wagged it sagely. "Well, you've allus been tellin' me that I got you out of your bed for nothing and I was imagining things when I thought me dog was ill."

"Yes," I said. "That's right."

"And I never believed you, did I? I wouldn't be told. Well now I know you were right all the time. I've been nobbut a fool and I'm right sorry for botherin' you all those nights."

"Oh, I shouldn't worry about that, Humphrey."

"Aye, but it's not right." He waved a hand toward his bright-faced, tail-wagging little dog. "Just look at her. Anybody can see there was never anythin' wrong with Myrtle tonight."

A Spot or Two
of Bother

———⟍○⟋———

I am never at my best in the early morning, especially the cold mornings you get in Yorkshire when a piercing wind sweeps down from the fells, finding its way inside clothing, nipping at noses and ears. It was a cheerless time, and a particularly bad time to be standing in this cobbled farmyard watching a beautiful horse dying because of my incompetence.

It had started at eight o'clock. Mr. Kettlewell telephoned as I was finishing my breakfast.

"I 'ave a fine big cart 'oss here and he's come out in spots."

"Really? What kind of spots?"

"Well, round and flat, and they're all over 'im."

"And it started quite suddenly?"

"Aye, he were right as rain last night."

"All right, I'll have a look at him right away." I

nearly rubbed my hands. Urticaria. It usually cleared up spontaneously, but an injection hastened the process and I had a new antihistamine drug to try out—it was said to be specific for this sort of thing. Anyway, it was the kind of situation where it was easy for the vet to look good. A nice start to the day.

In the fifties, the tractor had taken over most of the work on the farms, but there was still a fair number of draft horses around, and when I arrived at Mr. Kettlewell's place I realized that this one was something special.

The farmer was leading him from a loose box into the yard. A magnificent Shire, all of eighteen hands, with a noble head which he tossed proudly as he paced toward me. I appraised him with something like awe, taking in the swelling curve of the neck, the deep-chested body, the powerful limbs abundantly feathered above the massive feet.

"What a wonderful horse!" I gasped. "He's enormous!"

Mr. Kettlewell smiled with quiet pride. "Aye, he's a right smasher. I only bought 'im last month. I do like to have a good 'oss about."

He was a tiny man, elderly but sprightly, and one of my favorite farmers. He had to reach high to pat the huge neck and was nuzzled in return. "He's kind, too. Right quiet."

"Ah well, it's worth a lot when a horse is good-natured as well as good-looking." I ran my hand over the typical plaques in the skin. "Yes, this is urticaria, all right."

"What's that?"

"Sometimes it's called nettle rash. It's an allergic condition. He may have eaten something unusual, but it's often difficult to pinpoint the cause."

"Is it serious?"

"Oh no. I have an injection that'll soon put him right. He's well enough in himself, isn't he?"

"Aye, right as a bobbin."

"Good. Sometimes it upsets an animal, but this fellow's the picture of health."

As I filled my syringe with the antihistamine I felt that I had never spoken truer words. The big horse radiated health and well-being.

He did not move as I gave the injection, and I was about to put my syringe away when I had another thought. I had always used a proprietary preparation for urticaria and it had invariably worked. Maybe it would be a good idea to supplement the antihistamine, just to make sure. I wanted a good, quick cure for this splendid horse.

I trotted back to my car to fetch the old standby and injected the usual dose. Again the big animal paid no attention and the farmer laughed.

"By gaw, he doesn't mind, does 'e?"

I pocketed the syringe. "No, I wish all our patients were like him. He's a grand sort."

This, I thought, was vetting at its best. An easy, trouble-free case, a nice farmer and a docile patient who was a picture of equine beauty, a picture I could have looked at all day. I didn't want to go away although other calls were waiting. I just stood there, half listening to Mr. Kettlewell's chatter about the imminent lambing season.

"Ah well," I said at length, "I must be on my way." I was turning to go when I noticed that the farmer had fallen silent.

The silence lasted for a few moments, then, "He's dotherin' a bit," he said.

I looked at the horse. There was the faintest tremor in the muscles of the limbs. It was hardly visible, but as I watched, it began to spread upward, bit by bit, until the skin over the neck, body and rump began to quiver. It was very slight, but there was no doubt it was gradually increasing in intensity.

"What is it?" said Mr. Kettlewell.

"Oh, just a little reaction. It'll soon pass off." I was trying to sound airy, but I wasn't so sure.

With agonizing slowness the trembling developed into a generalized shaking of the entire frame and this steadily increased in violence as the farmer and I stood there in silence. I seemed to have been there a long time, trying to look calm and unworried, but I couldn't believe what I was seeing. This sudden inexplicable transition—there was no reason for it. My heart began to thump and my mouth turned dry as the shaking was replaced by great shuddering spasms which racked the horse's frame, and his eyes, so serene a short while ago, started from his head in terror, while foam began to drop from his lips. My mind raced. Maybe I shouldn't have mixed those injections, but it couldn't have this fearful effect. It was impossible.

As the seconds passed, I felt I couldn't stand much more of this. The blood hammered in my ears. Surely he would start to recover soon—he couldn't get worse.

I was wrong. Almost imperceptibly the huge animal began to sway. Only a little at first, then more and more until he was tilting from side to side like a mighty oak in a gale. Oh, dear God, he was going to go down and that would be the end. And that end had to come soon. Even the cobbles seemed to shake under my feet as the great horse crashed to the ground. For a few moments he lay there, stretched on his side, his feet pedaling convulsively, then he was still.

Well, that was it. I had killed this magnificent horse. It was impossible, unbelievable that a few minutes ago that animal had been standing there in all his strength and beauty and I had come along with my clever new medicines and now there he was, dead.

What was I going to say? I'm terribly sorry, Mr. Kettlewell, I just can't understand how this happened. My mouth opened, but nothing came out, not even a croak. And, as though looking at a picture from the outside I became aware of the square of farm buildings with the dark, snow-streaked fells rising behind under a lowering sky, of the biting wind, the farmer and myself, and the motionless body of the horse.

I felt chilled to the bone and miserable, but I had to say my piece. I took a long, quavering breath and was about to speak when the horse raised his head slightly. I said nothing, nor did Mr. Kettlewell, as the big animal eased himself onto his chest, looked around him for a few seconds, then got to his feet. He shook his head, then walked across to his master. The recovery was just as quick, just as incredible, as the devastating collapse, and he showed no ill effects from his crashing fall onto the cobbled yard.

The farmer reached up and patted the horse's neck. "You know, Mr. Herriot, them spots have nearly gone!"

I went over and had a look. "That's right. You can hardly see them now."

Mr. Kettlewell shook his head wonderingly. "Aye, well, it's a wonderful new treatment. But I'll tell tha summat. I hope you don't mind me sayin' this, but," he put his hand on my arm and looked up into my face, "ah think it's just a bit drastic."

I drove away from the farm and pulled up the car in the lee of a drystone wall. A great weariness had descended upon me. This sort of thing wasn't good for me. I was getting on in years now—well into my thirties—and I couldn't stand these shocks like I used to. I tipped the driving mirror down and had a look at myself. I was a bit pale, but not as ghastly white as I felt. Still, the feeling of guilt and bewilderment persisted, and with it the recurring thought that there must be easier ways of earning a living than as a country veterinary surgeon. Twenty-four hours a day, seven days a week, rough, dirty and peppered with traumatic incidents like that near catastrophe back there. I leaned back against the seat and closed my eyes.

When I opened them a few minutes later, the sun had broken through the clouds, bringing the green hillsides and the sparkling ridges of snow to vivid life, painting the rocky outcrops with gold. I wound down the window and breathed in the cold clean air drifting down, fresh and tangy, from the moorland high above.

Peace began to steal through me. Maybe I hadn't done anything wrong with Mr. Kettlewell's horse. Maybe antihistamines did sometimes cause these reactions. Anyway, as I started the engine and drove away, the old feeling began to well up in me and within moments it was running strong: it was good to be able to work with animals in this thrilling countryside; I was lucky to be a vet in the Yorkshire Dales.

There's Christmas—
and Christmas

This was a different kind of ringing. I had gone to sleep as the great bells in the church tower down the street pealed for the Christmas midnight mass, but this was a sharper, shriller sound.

It was difficult at first to shake off the mantle of unreality in which I had wrapped myself last night. Last night—Christmas Eve. It had been like a culmination of all the ideas I had ever held about Christmas—a flowering of emotions I had never experienced before. It had been growing in me since the afternoon call to a tiny village where the snow lay deep on the single street and on the walls and on the ledges of the windows where the lights on the tinseled trees glowed red and blue and gold; and as I left it in the dusk I drove beneath the laden branches of a group of dark

spruce as motionless as though they had been sketched against the white background of the fields.

When I reached Darrowby it was dark and around the marketplace the little shops were bright with decorations and the light from their windows fell in a soft yellow wash over the trodden snow of the cobbles. People, anonymously muffled, were hurrying about, doing their last-minute shopping, their feet slithering over the rounded stones.

I had known many Christmases in Scotland but they had taken second place to the New Year celebrations; there had been none of this air of subdued excitement which started days before with folk shouting good wishes, and colored lights winking on the lonely fellsides, and the farmers' wives plucking the fat geese, the feathers piled deep around their feet. And for fully two weeks you heard the children piping carols in the street then knocking on the door for sixpences. And best of all, last night the Methodist choir had sung out there, filling the night air with rich, thrilling harmony.

Before going to bed and just as the church bells began I closed the door of Skeldale House behind me and walked again into the marketplace. Nothing stirred now in the white square stretching smooth and cold and empty under the moon, and there was a Dickens look about the ring of houses and shops put together long before anybody thought of town planning; tall and short, fat and thin, squashed in crazily around the cobbles, their snow-burdened roofs jagged and uneven against the frosty sky.

As I walked back, the snow crunching under my feet, the bells clanging, the sharp air tingling in my nostrils, the wonder and mystery of Christmas enveloped me in a great wave. Peace on earth, goodwill toward men; the words became meaningful as never before and I saw myself suddenly as a tiny particle in the scheme of things; Darrowby, the farmers, the animals and me seemed for the first time like a warm, comfortable entity. I hadn't been drinking but I almost floated up the stairs to our bed-sitter.

Helen was still asleep and as I crawled between the

sheets beside her I was still wallowing in my Yuletide euphoria. There wouldn't be much work tomorrow; we'd have a long lie—maybe until nine—and then a lazy day, a glorious hiatus in our busy life. As I drifted into sleep it was as though I was surrounded by the smiling faces of my clients looking down at me with an all-embracing benevolence; and strangely I fancied I could hear singing, sweet and haunting, just like the Methodist choir—"God Rest Ye Merry Gentlemen . . ."

But now there was this other bell which wouldn't stop. Must be the alarm. But as I pawed at the clock the noise continued and I saw that it was six o'clock. It was the phone, of course. I lifted the receiver.

A metallic voice, crisp and very wide awake, jarred in my ear. "Is that the vet?"

"Yes, Herriot speaking," I mumbled.

"This is Brown, Willet Hill. I've got a cow down with milk fever. I want you here quick."

"Right, I'll see to it."

"Don't take ower long." Then a click at the far end.

I rolled onto my back and stared at the ceiling. So this was Christmas Day. The day when I was going to step out of the world for a spell and luxuriate in the seasonal spirit. I hadn't bargained for this fellow jerking me brutally back to reality. And not a word of regret or apology. No "sorry to get you out of bed" or anything else, never mind "Merry Christmas." It was just a bit hard.

Mr. Brown was waiting for me in the darkness of the farmyard. I had been to his place a few times before and as my headlights blazed on him I was struck, as always, by his appearance of perfect physical fitness. He was a gingery man of about forty with high cheekbones set in a sharp-featured, clear-skinned face. Red hair peeped from under a check cap and a faint auburn down covered his cheeks, his neck, the backs of his hands. It made me feel a bit more sleepy just to look at him.

He didn't say good morning but nodded briefly, then jerked his head in the direction of the byre. "She's in there" was all he said.

He watched in silence as I gave the injections and it wasn't until I was putting the empty bottles into my pocket that he spoke.

"Don't suppose I'll have to milk her today?"

"No," I replied. "Better leave the bag full."

"Anything special about feedin'?" Mr. Brown was very efficient. Always wanted to know every detail.

"No, she can have anything she likes when she wants it."

As we crossed the yard he halted suddenly and turned to face me. Could it be that he was going to ask me in for a nice hot cup of tea?

"You know," he said, as I stood ankle-deep in the

snow, the frosty air nipping at my ears. "I've had a few of these cases lately. Maybe there's summat wrong with my routine. Do you think I'm steaming up my cows too much?"

"It's quite possible." I hurried toward the car. One thing I wasn't going to do was deliver a lecture on animal husbandry at this moment.

My hand was on the door handle when he said, "I'll give you another ring if she's not up by dinnertime. And there's one other thing—that was a hell of a bill I had from you fellers last month, so tell your boss not to be so savage with 'is pen." Then he turned and walked quickly toward the house.

Well that was nice, I thought as I drove away. Not even thanks or good-bye, just a complaint and a promise to haul me away from my roast goose if necessary. A sudden wave of anger surged in me. Bloody farmers! There were some miserable devils among them. Mr. Brown had doused my festive feeling as effectively as if he had thrown a bucket of water over me. As I mounted the steps of Skeldale House the darkness had paled to a shivery gray. Helen met me in the passage. She was carrying a tray.

"I'm sorry, Jim," she said. "There's another urgent job. Siegfried's had to go out, too. But I've got a cup of coffee and some fried bread for you. Come in and sit down—you've got time to eat it before you go."

I sighed. It was going to be just another day after

all. "What's this about, Helen?" I asked, sipping the coffee.

"It's old Mr. Kirby," she replied. "He's very worried about his nanny goat."

"Nanny goat!"

"Yes, he says she's choking."

"Choking! How the heck can she be choking?" I shouted.

"I really don't know. And I wish you wouldn't shout at me, Jim. It's not my fault."

In an instant I was engulfed by shame. Here I was, in a bad temper, taking it out on my wife. It is a common reaction for vets to blame the hapless person who passes on an unwanted message but I am not proud of it. I held out my hand and Helen took it.

"I'm sorry," I said and finished the coffee sheepishly. My feeling of goodwill was at a very low ebb.

Mr. Kirby was a retired farmer, but he had sensibly taken a cottage with a bit of land where he kept enough stock to occupy his time—a cow, a few pigs and his beloved goats. He had always had goats, even when he was running his dairy herd; he had a thing about them.

The cottage was in a village high up the dale. Mr. Kirby met me at the gate.

"Ee, lad," he said. "I'm right sorry to be bothering you this early in the morning and Christmas an' all, but I didn't have no choice. Dorothy's real bad."

He led the way to a stone shed which had been converted into a row of pens. Behind the wire of one of them a large white Saanen goat peered out at us anxiously and as I watched her she gulped, gave a series of retching coughs, then stood trembling, saliva drooling from her mouth.

The farmer turned to me, wide-eyed. "You see, I had to get you out, didn't I? If I left her till tomorrow she'd be a goner."

"You're right, Mr. Kirby," I replied. "You couldn't leave her. There's something in her throat."

We went into the pen and as the old man held the goat against the wall I tried to open her mouth. She didn't like it very much and as I pried her jaws apart she startled me with a loud, long-drawn, human-sounding cry. It wasn't a big mouth but I have a small hand and I poked a finger deep into the pharynx, avoiding the sharp back teeth.

There was something there all right. I could just touch it but I couldn't get hold of it. Then the animal began to throw her head about and I had to come out; I stood there, saliva dripping from my hand, looking thoughtfully at Dorothy.

After a few moments I turned to the farmer. "You know, this is a bit baffling. I can feel something in the back of her throat, but it's soft—like cloth. I'd been expecting to find a bit of twig, or something sharp sticking in there—it's funny what a goat will pick up when she's pottering around outside. But if it's cloth, what the heck is holding it here? Why hasn't she swallowed it down?"

"Aye, it's a rum 'un, isn't it?" The old man ran a gentle hand along the animal's back. "Do you think she'll get rid of it herself? Maybe it'll just slip down?"

"No, I don't. It's stuck fast, God knows how, but it is. And I've got to get it out soon because she's beginning to blow up. Look there." I pointed to the goat's gas-filled stomach and as I did so, Dorothy began another paroxysm of coughs which seemed almost to tear her apart.

Mr. Kirby looked at me with a mute appeal, but just at that moment I didn't see what I could do. Then

I opened the door of the pen. "I'm going to get my flashlight from the car. Maybe I'll see something to explain this."

The old man held the flashlight as I once more pulled the goat's mouth open and again heard the curious child-like wailing. It was when the animal was in full cry that I noticed something under the tongue—a thin, dark band.

"I can see what's holding the thing now," I cried. "It's hooked round the tongue with string or something." Carefully I pushed my forefinger under the band and began to pull.

It wasn't string. It began to stretch as I pulled carefully at it . . . like elastic. Then it stopped stretching and I felt a real resistance . . . whatever was in the throat was beginning to move. I kept up a gentle traction and very slowly the mysterious obstruction came sliding up over the back of the tongue and into the mouth, and when it came within reach I let go the elastic, grabbed the sodden mass and hauled it forth. It seemed as if there was no end to it—a long snake of dripping material nearly two feet long—but at last I had it out onto the straw of the pen.

Mr. Kirby seized it and held it up and as he unraveled the mass wonderingly he gave a sudden cry.

"God 'elp us, it's me summer drawers!"

"Your *what*?"

"Me summer drawers. Ah don't like them long

johns when weather gets warmer and I allus change into these little short 'uns. Missus was havin' a clear-out afore the end of t'year and she didn't know whether to wash 'em or mek them into dusters. She washed them at t'finish and Dorothy must have got 'em off the line." He held up the tattered shorts and regarded them ruefully. "By gaw, they'd seen better days, but I reckon Dorothy's fettled them this time."

Then his body began to shake silently, a few low giggles escaped from him and finally he gave a great shout of laughter. It was an infectious laugh and I joined in as I watched him. He went on for quite a long time and when he had finished he was leaning weakly against the wire netting.

"Me poor awd drawers," he gasped, then leaned over and patted the goat's head. "But as long as you're all right, lass, I'm not worried."

"Oh, she'll be okay," I pointed to her left flank. "You can see her stomach's going down already." As I spoke, Dorothy belched pleasurably and began to nose interestedly at her hayrack.

The farmer gazed at her fondly. "Isn't that grand to see! She's ready for her grub again. And if she hadn't got her tongue round the elastic that lot would have gone right down and killed her."

"I really don't think it would, you know," I said. "It's amazing what ruminants can carry around in their stomachs. I once found a bicycle tire inside a cow when I was operating for something else. The tire didn't seem to be bothering her in the least."

"I see." Mr. Kirby rubbed his chin. "So Dorothy might have wandered around with me drawers inside her for years."

"It's possible. You'd never have known what became of them."

"By gaw, that's right," Mr. Kirby said, and for a moment I thought he was going to start giggling again, but he mastered himself and seized my arm. "But I don't know what I'm keeping you out here for, lad. You must come in and have a bit o' Christmas cake."

Inside the tiny living room of the cottage I was ushered to the best chair by the fireside where two rough logs blazed and crackled.

"Bring cake out for Mr. Herriot, Mother," the farmer cried as he rummaged in the pantry. He reappeared with a bottle of whiskey at the same time as his wife bustled in carrying a cake thickly laid with icing and ornamented with colored spangles, toboggans, reindeers.

Mr. Kirby unscrewed the stopper. "You know, Mother, we're lucky to have such men as this to come out on a Christmas mornin' to help us."

"Aye, we are that." The old lady cut a thick slice of the cake and placed it on a plate by the side of an enormous wedge of Wensleydale cheese.

Her husband meanwhile was pouring my drink.

Yorkshire men are amateurs with whiskey and there was something delightfully untutored in the way he was sloshing it into the glass as if it were lemonade; he would have filled it to the brim if I hadn't stopped him.

Drink in hand, cake on knee, I looked across at the farmer and his wife who were sitting in upright kitchen chairs watching me with quiet benevolence. The two faces had something in common—a kind of beauty. You would find faces like that only in the country; deeply wrinkled and weathered, clear-eyed, alight with cheerful serenity.

I raised my glass. "A happy Christmas to you both."

The old couple nodded and replied smilingly. "And the same to you, Mr. Herriot."

"Aye, and thanks again, lad," said Mr. Kirby. "We're right grateful to you for runnin' out here to save awd Dorothy. We've maybe mucked up your day for you but it would've mucked up ours if we'd lost the old lass, wouldn't it, Mother?"

"Don't worry, you haven't spoiled anything for me," I said. "In fact, you've made me realize again that it really is Christmas." And as I looked around the little room with the decorations hanging from the low-beamed ceiling I could feel the emotions of last night surging slowly back, a warmth creeping through me that had nothing to do with the whiskey.

I took a bite of the cake and followed it with a

moist slice of cheese. When I had first come to York-shire I had been aghast when offered this unheard-of combination, but time had brought wisdom and I had discovered that the mixture when chewed boldly together was exquisite; and, strangely, I had also found that there was nothing more suitable for wash-ing it finally over the tonsils than a draft of raw whiskey.

"You don't mind t'wireless, Mr. Herriot?" Mrs. Kirby asked. "We always like to have it on Christmas morning to hear t'old hymns but I'll turn it off if you like."

"No, please leave it, it sounds grand." I turned to look at the old radio with its chipped wooden veneer, the ornate scroll-work over the worn fabric; it must have been one of the earliest models and it gave off a tinny sound, but the singing of the church choir was none the less sweet . . . "Hark the Herald Angels Sing"—flooding the little room, mingling with the splutter of the logs and the soft voices of the old people.

They showed me a picture of their son, who was a policeman over in Houlton, and their daughter, who was married to a neighboring farmer. They were bringing their grandchildren up for Christmas dinner as they always did and Mrs. Kirby opened a box and ran a hand over the long row of crackers. The choir started on "Once in Royal David's City." I finished my whiskey and put up only feeble resistance as the farmer plied the bottle again. Through the small window I could see the bright berries of a holly tree pushing through their covering of snow.

It was really a shame to have to leave here and it was sadly that I drained my glass for the second time and scooped up the last crumbs of cake and icing from my plate.

Mr. Kirby came out with me and at the gate of the cottage he stopped and held out his hand.

"Thank ye, lad, I'm right grateful," he said. "And all the very best to you."

For a moment the rough dry palm rasped against mine, then I was in the car, starting the engine. I looked at my watch; it was still only half past nine but the first early sunshine was sparkling from a sky of palest blue.

Beyond the village the road climbed steeply, then curved around the rim of the valley in a wide arc, and it was here you came suddenly upon the whole great expanse of the Plain of York spread out almost at your feet. I always slowed down here and there was always something different to see, but today the vast checkerboard of fields and farms and woods stood out with a clarity I had never seen before. Maybe it was because this was a holiday and down there no factory chimney smoked, no trucks belched fumes, but the distance was magically foreshortened in the clear, frosty air and I felt I could reach out and touch the familiar landmarks far below.

I looked back at the enormous white billows and folds of the fells, crowding close, one upon another into the blue distance, every crevice uncannily defined, the highest summits glittering where the sun touched them. I could see the village with the Kirbys' cottage at the end. I had found Christmas and peace and goodwill and everything back there.

Farmers? They were the salt of the earth.